MYSTERIOUS CREATURES

MYSTERIOUS CREATURES

The Truth Behind the Legends

David Alderton
Akara Heart

BLOOMSBURY ACADEMIC
NEW YORK • LONDON • OXFORD • NEW DELHI • SYDNEY

BLOOMSBURY ACADEMIC
Bloomsbury Publishing Inc, 1359 Broadway, 12th Floor, New York, NY 10018, USA
Bloomsbury Publishing Plc, 50 Bedford Square, London, WC1B 3DP, UK
Bloomsbury Publishing Ireland, 29 Earlsfort Terrace, Dublin 2, D02 AY28, Ireland

BLOOMSBURY, BLOOMSBURY ACADEMIC and the Diana logo
are trademarks of Bloomsbury Publishing Plc

First published in the United States of America 2026

Cover design: Devin Watson
Cover images: Devin Watson

Bloomsbury Publishing Inc does not have any control over, or responsibility for, any
third-party websites referred to or in this book. All internet addresses given in this
book were correct at the time of going to press. The author and publisher regret
any inconvenience caused if addresses have changed or sites have ceased
to exist, but can accept no responsibility for any such changes.

A catalog record for this book is available from the Library of Congress.

ISBN: HB: 978-1-5381-9386-0
ePDF: 979-8-8818-6173-5
eBook: 978-1-5381-9387-7

Typeset by Integra Software Services Pvt. Ltd.
Printed and bound in the United States of America

For product safety related questions contact productsafety@bloomsbury.com

To find out more about our authors and books visit www.bloomsbury.com
and sign up for our newsletters.

Contents

Acknowledgments

The authors would particularly like to thank Christen Karniski for her patience and encouragement; our super agent, Isabel Atherton of Creative Authors in New York; plus the photographers for the use of their images (see List of Figures on the following pages).

Figures

Introduction

Scary locations: the mind can play tricks, with stories
often developing and spreading in the area.
Photo courtesy Raggedstone/www.shutterstock.com 1

An okapi: a species only officially discovered at the start
of the twentieth century but known previously from native stories.
Photo courtesy Jiri Hrebicek/www.shutterstock.com 3

1. The Quest for the Unicorn

The typical popular appearance of a unicorn.
Photo courtesy Annabell Gsoedi/www.shutterstock.com 7

The figurehead on the HMS *Unicorn*—a restored forty-six-gun navy
warship built in 1824, now located in Scotland.
Photo courtesy Atmosphere1/www.shutterstock.com 13

A narwhal skull with horn attached: the source of the unicorn horn.
Photo courtesy Michelle van Dijk/www.shutterstock.com 23

A living narwhal, revealing its distinctive horn.
Photo courtesy Saifullahphotographer/www.shutterstock.com 24

2. Mermaids and Mermen

A typical mermaid. *Photo courtesy PeopleImages.com—
Yuri A/www.shutterstock.com* 31

INTRODUCTION

Scary locations: the mind can play tricks, with stories often developing and spreading in the area.
Photo courtesy Raggedstone/www.shutterstock.com

During the late 1500s, an English traveler named Andrew Battel was in central Africa, being one of the first Europeans to journey widely across the continent. In due course, he returned to England and wrote about his travels. Battel described two fearsome animals, both of which were considered by the local people to be extremely aggressive. The bigger one was called "pongo," while its smaller counterpart was known as "engeco." Pongos were said to be taller than men, with hairy bodies and human-like faces. They lived in groups and would attack and kill people, as well as driving off elephants with clubs. Battel was told that pongos could never be captured alive, as they had the strength of at least ten men. On occasions, they would kidnap children, who were never seen again.

The Reality Is Less Frightening

The truth behind Battel's frightening descriptions did not start to emerge until centuries later, during the 1850s, when two missionaries obtained skulls of these monstrous creatures from the country of Gabon. Today, we recognize engecos as chimpanzees (*Pan troglodytes*), while the pongo is better known as the lowland gorilla (*Gorilla gorilla*). These shy, retiring great apes feed largely on plants and berries—far removed in behavior from the way they were described to Battel.

Similar tales surrounded the discovery of the related mountain gorilla (*Gorilla beringei*), which is now an endangered species. The natives told how these apes, which they called "ngagi" or "ngila," would hug women so tightly with their strong arms that they could crush them to death. In this case, it was only as recently as 1902 that these gorillas, standing up to 6.3 feet (1.95 m) in height and weighing more than 600 pounds (270 kg), first became known outside Africa, when a skin obtained by Captain Oscar von Beringe was sent to the Berlin Zoological Museum for study.

These events show how folk stories can so easily develop, as fact mixes with fiction in the absence of accurate knowledge, causing the truth to become obscured. Could this also apply in the case of North America's hidden or "cryptid hominoid" (literally meaning a "hidden man-like creature") known both as Sasquatch and Bigfoot?

Much More to Discover

Even today, the world is a place of mystery. Tempting though it may be to assume that we have identified virtually all the species that share the planet with us, this is not only far from the truth, but in fact, according to most scientists, we only know a minority of them. Although just over two million

An okapi: a species only officially discovered at the start of the twentieth century but known previously from native stories.
Photo courtesy Jiri Hrebicek/www.shutterstock.com

have already been classified, meaning they have a scientific name and their identifying characteristics have been described, there could, based on some estimates, be more than four times as many—some eight million creatures—alive today and still to be recognized by science. Many of these will be invertebrates, living in remote, inaccessible areas, such as high up in the trees of the world's rainforests, but even now, over recent decades, there have been some amazing discoveries of new large vertebrates, and almost certainly, there are others still out there, waiting to be found.

Seeking the Truth

Today, with access to the internet, it is very easy to gain information about an animal with a few clicks of the mouse, but in the past, of course, this was simply not possible. Knowledge was built up very slowly over time, and sharing it was difficult in the days before printing. Everything had to be written out and copied by hand, which was a slow and laborious process. It made it hard to disseminate new information quickly. Even so, this did not curtail the human imagination, as reflected by the tales told about various creatures. Tales that were likely to fascinate and sometimes even scare the audience listening to them. Like all good stories, they also typically contained a certain degree of truth as well.

The subjects covered in this book all have a long history, dating back many centuries. There have been times in the past when they were definitely thought to be living creatures, and even today, we are not entirely sure as to whether they all are mythological.

Those who investigate such claims are known as cryptozoologists, a term that reflects the fact that the existence of such creatures is uncertain. A zoologist is someone who studies animals, and the "crypto" added to this name, is derived from the ancient Greek word *kryptós*, which literally means "hidden," indicating they are focused on species currently unknown to science—hidden animals.

The name comes from a pioneer researcher in the field during the 1950s named Ivan Sanderson, but it nevertheless remains a controversial branch of zoology. The aim of cryptozoologists is to try to apply scientific investigative methods to animal mysteries. In recent years, this has become easier, thanks to significant advances in investigative tools and techniques, which have actually upended traditional scientific views in some cases. For example, DNA studies reveal that particular populations of animals, even in the case of large animals like giraffes, previously grouped together on the basis of their similarity in appearance, have now been shown to belong to more than one species. This has major conservation implications.

Back from the Dead

Remarkable and often totally unexpected finds of unknown species have also been made over the past century—with perhaps the most noteworthy being that of the coelacanth (*Latimeria chalumnae*). Recorded only from the fossil record, a living example of this fish was caught in 1938 in the depths of the ocean near the Comoros Islands, close to Madagascar off the southwest coast of Africa. It was spotted by chance, in a trawler's catch, by museum curator Marjorie Courtenay-Latimer.

She sought confirmation of the fish's identity from J. L. B. Smith, a fish scientist (known as an ichthyologist), who was based at Rhodes University in South Africa. He ultimately named the fish after her. Since then, a number of other coelacanths have been found in this area, some sixty-six million years after the group was believed to have died out. Perhaps even more remarkably, a totally separate population, representing a second unknown species, was located off the coast of Asia in 1998, becoming known as the Indonesian coelacanth (*Latimeria menadoensis*).

Other Finds Waiting to Be Made

So could it be that there are other animals still awaiting discovery? Without a doubt. New technology is helping to reveal and track the presence of such species. The saola, which features as part of the unicorn story (see Chapter 1), was observed on a trail camera during 2013 in the mountainous central area of Vietnam. This was the first sighting of this exceptionally rare and critically endangered species in the twenty-first century. Prior to this, it had last been spotted on a trail cam photograph during 1999 in Laos. Without such technology, the saola would have been almost totally unobserved since its discovery in 1992, raising serious doubts about its continued survival.

This book focuses on some of the most widely known mysterious creatures, all of which have been considered to be living animals of different types at various times in history. The question is: could they actually exist, and if not, what may have given rise to stories about them that have lasted down through the centuries? Join us on a voyage of discovery to find the truth behind the legends, and prepare to be surprised!

1

THE QUEST FOR
THE UNICORN

The typical popular appearance of a unicorn.
Photo courtesy Annabell Gsoedi/www.shutterstock.com

Thousands of years ago, people understood very little about animals and the natural world. It also wasn't possible to share knowledge easily, because although information could be written down, there was no printing of any kind. This meant that discoveries could not be circulated easily; manuscripts had to be copied by hand and this was very time-consuming work. The number of people who could read was very limited too.

Life was also completely different in many other ways from today, with people often spending their entire lives in the villages where they were born. Back then, travel was extremely difficult, not to mention dangerous. Those who ventured to foreign countries often returned with amazing tales that frequently became more exaggerated every time they were told, especially if money was at stake—as became the case with unicorns.

The Earliest References

What is believed to be the very first evidence suggesting the existence of the unicorn dates back more than four thousand years. It comes in the form of wax seals that were used to close documents. Hot liquid sealing wax was tipped onto the folded paper, with the seal then being pressed down into it. The wax hardened in place as it cooled and contained the image from the seal. This then had to be broken to read the message, showing the document had been opened.

The design on these seals was more reminiscent of a bull, rather than the horse-like unicorn we know today. The single horn was nevertheless placed in the middle of the animal's forehead, rather than being on either side of the head. These seals originated from an area of southern Asia, which includes part of today's countries of India and Pakistan.

The Appearance of Unicorns

The first definite description of unicorns that we know about is approximately 2,400 years old. This account was included in a book titled *Indica*, written by a Greek doctor named Ctesias. He was born in 400 BCE and had previously lived in what was then Persia (now Iran), where he had worked as the official court physician to King Darius II for seventeen years.

While Ctesias was in Persia, he had collected a lot of information from many different sources, including people who had traveled widely farther east.

When he returned to Greece, he wrote *Indica* about what was then this rather mysterious area of southern Asia, which is roughly equivalent to what we know as India today, using the knowledge that he had gained from such contacts.

In *Indica*, Ctesias provided detailed information about the unicorn. He described it as a wild ass, which was about the size or possibly even larger than a horse. Asses do look very similar to horses, but their body shape tends to be slightly different, and they have bigger ears. Yet there were also clearly distinctive features that Ctesias referred to, which set unicorns apart from any known member of the horse, ass, and zebra family. He referred to them as being multicolored, with a bright red head offset against a white body, while their eyes were bluish in color.

The most unique aspect of their appearance was, however, their horn. This was positioned in the center of the forehead, and it was a cubit long, according to Ctesias. The cubit is an ancient measure of length that was based on the distance from your elbow to the tip of your middle finger, roughly equivalent to 1.5 feet (45 cm) today.

The colors of the unicorn's horn itself were striking. While the base, which Ctesias noted as being two palms in width, was white, this was followed by a black area in the middle. The upper part of the horn, including the tip, was a stunning shade of flaming red.

Ctesias's account of the unicorn was very matter-of-fact. He clearly did not believe that he was describing a mythical animal, but one that was real, even though he had not seen it himself. He also noted how unicorns were said to be able to outpace a horse when running.

The Unicorn's Range

Although Ctesias described the land where the unicorn could be found as "Indica," the exact locality that he had in mind is unclear. It has been suggested that he may have been referring to the Tibetan Plateau.

We do know that the homeland of the only surviving wild horse— Przewalski's horse (*Equus ferus przewalskii*)—was in this region of Asia, on the central steppes. At that stage in history, during Ctesias's time, it was probably relatively common, but the wild population was wiped out by hunting in the 1900s. Luckily, though, it has been saved from extinction by captive breeding. A now thriving population of these unique wild horses was reintroduced in the 1990s to Mongolia.

Subsequent Accounts

Following Ctesias, it was another Greek writer, Aristotle (384–322 BCE), who continued writing about the unicorn. He included it in his large work *Historia animalium*, which was produced in ten volumes, but he did acknowledge that it had never been seen.

As part of his classification, dividing animals into related groups, Aristotle also highlighted the fact that the single-horned unicorn, which he referred to as the Indian ass, had a distinctive characteristic. It could be recognized by having a single hoof on each foot, rather than the typical "split" or cloven hooves of other horned animals such as cattle or goats, indicating that it was a type of horse.

Increasing curiosity about the natural world soon resulted in more attempts being made to gain a better understanding of the relationships between different types of animals and to group them accordingly. This marked the start of a process that has continued through to the present day and underpins the branch of science called *classification*. One of the key aspects of this system is that for an animal to be given a scientific name, which is always written in italics, a specimen of the animal must be available for study in a museum. Since this has never happened with a unicorn, it therefore does not have a formal scientific name.

There are just twenty-five known copies of Aristotle's original manuscript surviving today. It was undoubtedly never common, and given the shortage of written material back then, it is perhaps not surprising that the influence of both Ctesias and Aristotle remained significant and essentially unchallenged for centuries. Later Roman writers were clearly very familiar with their works, and it was at this stage that the confusion over the unicorn's identity becomes ever deeper.

Pliny the Elder (23–79 CE) compiled a large summary about all the animals in the known world, which was titled *Naturalis historia*, and this included an animal from India he called the monoceros. It was said to have a head resembling that of a stag, feet similar to those of an elephant, and a tail like a pig's, all combined with the body of a horse. But undoubtedly, the monoceros's most distinctive feature, according to Pliny, was the single black horn that protruded from its forehead and grew to a length of approximately two cubits, or 3 feet (90 cm).

The monoceros was reputedly not only a fierce animal, but also impossible to catch alive. Although "monoceros" was a Greek word, it was not long before the name of this mysterious and elusive creature was translated into Latin as "unicornis," meaning "one-horned," from which we have ultimately gained the description of "unicorn" into our language today.

An Inner Meaning?

As civilization spread more widely across Europe from the third to seventh centuries CE, in part because of the collapse of the Roman Empire, there was a rise of interest in what have become known as bestiaries. These were books about animals produced in the form of illustrated manuscripts.

The most significant bestiary, in terms of the unicorn, is *Physiologus*. No one knows who wrote this work. The title translates as "naturalist"—meaning someone who has an expert insight into the natural world. But the text went beyond a simple description of the animal: instead, the stories were also allegorical, meaning that such accounts often carried a deeper, underlying message, which was linked with rebirth in the case of the unicorn.

Physiologus proved to be so popular that it was soon being translated from the original Greek version into a number of other different languages including Ethiopic, Armenian, and Anglo-Saxon (from which English itself developed), and these editions continued to be copied and reproduced for thousands of years, right up until the thirteenth century. This was therefore a very important work as far as the study of natural history was concerned. It also featured the phoenix (see Chapter 4).

In turn, *Physiologus* provided the inspiration for a range of other bestiaries. These featured both living and mythical animals and drew heavily on the works of earlier writers like Aristotle and other classical scholars, which partly helps to explain why the unicorn appears to be prominent in them.

Bestiaries are usually beautifully illustrated, featuring a wide range of animals, although the portrayals themselves are frequently not very accurate. This is because many of the living animals included had never been seen in life by those painting them. They could only rely on other descriptions and previous portrayals for guidance.

As a result, lions, for example, vary widely in appearance, with the mane of male lions being more accurately portrayed in some cases than others. Those animals which were better known in Europe, like bears, were generally shown as more realistic than others, such as elephants. Unsurprisingly perhaps, featured unicorns also display considerable variation in style, sometimes being portrayed with a goat-like beard and appearance for example, rather than having the profile of a horse.

Unicorns were not the only horned example of imaginary animals that featured in bestiaries. There was another called the yale or centicore, which in this case had a pair of horns. It differed from other horned animals, however, in that these were said to be able to swivel, so it typically had one horn directed forward, while the other pointed over its back. It was a formidable combatant if threatened, as it could use either horn. This resulted in the yale featuring quite often as a symbol in medieval heraldry.

How to Catch a Unicorn

In *Physiologus*, it was reported that unicorns were able to run very fast, which made them difficult to catch, quite apart from their fierce nature. As a general rule, only maidens could catch unicorns and tame them. In fact, a unicorn would often approach a maiden who was sitting on her own in a forest and fall asleep in her lap.

According to the author of *Physiologus*, this was a ruse used by hunters to capture a unicorn alive and lead it to their king, or in later versions of this tale, even kill it to obtain its horn. They would use a maiden as a decoy to draw the unicorn out and calm it down.

Although lions were generally believed not to be able to overcome unicorns with their fierce, brave natures, there were said to be various ways in which a lion could nevertheless get the better of its adversary. This idea came from a document reputedly written by an Ethiopian king called Prester John.

Ethiopia, lying in northeastern Africa, was an important trading center at that time and had established an empire. But while the information within this document became widely known in European court circles in the 1100s, whether the king himself ever existed is open to serious doubt.

Nevertheless, it was believed that there were unicorns present in this African country, and they would sometimes kill lions with their horn. Yet when a unicorn was tired, it rested under the shade of a tree, giving the lion a chance to overcome its deadly enemy by creeping up behind the tree. The unicorn would then charge at the lion, but when exhausted, it could misjudge its strike. If this happened, its horn became impaled deep within the tree,

The figurehead on the HMS Unicorn—*a restored forty-six-gun navy warship built in 1824, now located in Scotland.*
Photo courtesy Atmosphere1/www.shutterstock.com

leaving the unicorn unable to free itself. As a result, the lion then had the opportunity to kill its trapped rival.

This belief soon took hold in Europe, becoming widely accepted as the way to catch a unicorn. It features in "The Brave Little Tailor," a story in *Grimms' Fairy Tales*. This collection of traditional folk tales was compiled by brothers Jacob and Wilhelm Grimm and first appeared in 1812. In this case, the unicorn is captured by running into a tree in a similar way, impaling its horn in the wood. Even Shakespeare referred to this method of tricking a unicorn in his play *Julius Caesar*.

Ongoing Enmity

There was certainly a deep rivalry between unicorns and lions, dating back over countless centuries. It is unclear how or why this arose in the first place. Perhaps it was the result of a clash between the king of beasts—in the figure of the lion—and the brave, untamed nature of the unicorn?

Encounters between the two date back almost to the start of the unicorn story, to the ancient Palace of Forty Pillars built by Darius I in Persepolis, although it was not finished before his death. Instead, his son, who assumed the throne as King Darius II, completed the construction process, and it was here of course that Ctesias worked as the court physician.

There are various stone reliefs decorating this palace that survive to the present day showing a lion attacking an animal with a single horn. The animal cannot be identified clearly but reflects a combination of the features of a goat, a bull, and an antelope, depending on the location, with the horn in all cases being suggestive of a unicorn.

The battle between the lion and the unicorn has continued down the centuries, right through to the present day, as is reflected by the UK's Royal Coat of Arms, which shows both animals together. Although this might suggest the lion and unicorn have forged a bond, even here they are rivals. The lion represents England, while the free-spirited unicorn stands for the people of Scotland.

This coat of arms was created in 1603, when James VI, king of Scotland, became king of England as well, under the title of James I. Nevertheless, rather than being unified, there is a subtle difference between the designs used in the two countries even today. The Royal Coat of Arms of Scotland portrays both animals wearing crowns, with the unicorn (representing Scotland) being on the left. In the English version, however, only the lion is crowned, with their positions being reversed.

This use of a lion and unicorn in a coat of arms together is not unique to the United Kingdom, however, as both animals feature in the coat of arms of the Canadian provinces of Newfoundland and Labrador, for example, with the lion again wearing the crown. They are also paired in the coat of arms for the Slovakian town of Vrútky, although in this case, the lion is portrayed without a crown.

The enmity between the two animals is also featured in the popular collection of *Mother Goose* nursery rhymes. These rhymes were compiled by the French writer Charles Perrault in the 1690s, although the actual origin of "The Lion and the Unicorn" rhyme set out below is unclear:

The Lion and the Unicorn
were fighting for the crown:
The Lion beat the Unicorn
All around the town.
Some gave them white bread,
And some gave them brown:
Some gave them plum cake
and drummed them out of town.

This nursery rhyme clearly provided inspiration for the author Lewis Carroll, however, as it then features in his classic work *Alice Through the Looking-Glass*, published in 1871. Alice repeats this particular rhyme and watches the animals fighting in front of the king, while the unicorn asks her for some plum cake!

A Significant Find

There are other meanings attached to the use of the lion and unicorn in heraldry. It is clear that while the lion represents strength, the unicorn stands for chivalry. This is reflected in a remarkable series of six tapestries, which have become known as *The Lady and the Unicorn* tapestries.

The tapestries are a mystery in terms of their origins, as no one today is certain where they were made, let alone who commissioned them. It seems likely, however, that they were created in the city of Flanders (now part of Belgium) and may have been made for a wealthy French lawyer and royal adviser named Jean Le Viste. They have been dated to about 1500, which we do know was at the end of Le Viste's life.

The tapestries themselves are full of symbolism, not just in terms of the animals that are shown in them, but also with regard to the plants as well. Five of the six portray the senses—touch, taste, smell, hearing, and sight. In the case of the Touch tapestry, as an example, the maiden featured is seen holding the unicorn's horn, whereas in the case of Sight, the unicorn is portrayed kneeling alongside her, viewing its reflection in the mirror. In all cases, the lion is shown on the right-hand side of the noblewoman, with the unicorn on the left.

What stands out, however, is the fact that in the sixth tapestry, which is clearly different from the other five, the courtly love motto *À Mon Seul Désir* (translating literally from the French as "My only desire" or "My own free will") is clearly incorporated, above a blue tent. The noblewoman is opening a box of jewels, while sitting on a raised bench next to her on a lavishly embroidered cushion is a small dog. The lion and the unicorn are in their usual positions, on either side of her, and a mischievous monkey can also be seen. The unicorn in this case has a goat-like beard and is clearly cloven-hooved. This particular scene is suggestive of a marriage ceremony, given the gold brocade dress that the lady is wearing.

Rare Survivors

These beautiful tapestries are very rare survivors from the medieval period, and in fact, they were nearly lost. They were only rediscovered in 1841 in Boussac Castle, located in central France. Here the wool and silk from which they are made were under threat from a combination of damp and mold. The tapestries had already suffered some damage before being acquired in 1863 by Edmond Du Sommerard, who was the curator of the Musée de Cluny in Paris.

After being fully restored, they can still be seen there in the museum today, which specializes in medieval art of all types. More recently, in 1971, a special garden was also created in the grounds of this ancient priory, reflecting a unicorn forest inspired by the plants portrayed in these tapestries.

A Religious Significance

By this stage in European history, the unicorn had gained an allegorical importance in the early Christian church. This meant that the basic story shown in these tapestries also had a symbolic and deeper meaning, especially to people of that period. The unicorn's return to life mirrored the resurrection of Christ after his crucifixion and death, while the presence of the maiden undoubtedly corresponded to that of the Virgin Mary. There is another set of tapestries with a similar message from the same period in history purchased and restored in 1922 by John D. Rockefeller. These are now on display in the Met Cloisters in New York City.

At one level, therefore, the tapestries portray a strong Christian religious faith, but they also reflect courtly love—a brave knight (as portrayed by the unicorn again) seeking to win the affection of a virtuous noble lady. There are various fertility symbols included in the designs as well, such as pomegranate seeds, plus wild orchids, suggesting a possible marriage blessed by children.

It mattered not to medieval people that they had never seen or encountered a unicorn; it was known by them to symbolize bravery. During this era, when the majority of people were illiterate, the ability to tell stories about life and communicate through pictures was very important.

This type of messaging was well recognized, with wall paintings showing scenes from the Bible (the vast majority of which have now been lost) being commonly included on the walls of churches during that period for the same reason. The visual clues and meanings within these tapestries would undoubtedly have been very much clearer to onlookers at that stage in history than they are to us at first glance today. We tend to see things more literally nowadays, relying also on accompanying words to expand our understanding of a scene, in a way that was not possible for the majority of people back then.

Unicorns with Wings

Apart from ordinary unicorns, there are also accounts of some that have the ability to fly. Winged unicorns are known under a variety of different names, including, rather confusingly, alicorns, which is the same term used to describe the unicorn's distinctive spiraled horn. They are also known as pegacorns, which derives from a combination of "Pegasus" (the winged horse—see below) and "unicorn." Another description used for them is cerapter, which comes from the words *keras* meaning "horn," and *pteros* meaning "wings."

The earliest evidence of flying unicorns comes from the ancient Assyrian Empire, being in the form of seals, which date back to about 400 BCE. These, alongside winged bulls, appear to have been viewed as a representation of evil at that stage.

Pegasus: The Winged Horse

According to Greek legend, Pegasus's father was the god Poseidon. His beautiful mother, Medusa, had been turned into a monstrous, fearsome gorgon by the goddess Athena, with writhing snakes representing her hair. Medusa was known to be able to turn people into stone with her stare. Pegasus and his twin brother, Chrysaor, emerged out of her blood after she had been killed by the brave warrior Perseus.

Pegasus was unmistakably part horse, white in color but lacking the distinctive horn of a unicorn, with single hooves on each foot. His wings were covered in feathers, just like those of a bird. Being able to fly allowed him to travel far and wide, and wherever he landed, touching the ground with a hoof, so it was said, a stream would spring from the earth. The most famous of these is the Hippocrene, or "horse spring" on Mount Helicon in Greece. In fact, the first part of the name "Pegasus" actually comes from the word *pēgē*, which means "spring" or "well."

As is the case with unicorns, Pegasus was hard to tame and never wore a saddle. But he was finally captured by the Greek hero Bellerophon, using a magical golden bridle obtained from Athena. With the protection of the bridle, the pair then defeated the chimera—a creature made of the parts of different animals, whose appearance was said to be based on a lion with some goat-like features and a tail that could morph into a snake.

In his roles as king of the gods and the god of thunder, Zeus ruled from Mount Olympus. When Bellerophon attempted to fly on Pegasus to this mountain, with the aim of becoming a god himself, Zeus became very angry. He sent an irritating gadfly to bite Pegasus, causing him to rear up, which in turn resulted in Bellerophon falling off and tumbling to his death.

Acknowledging Pegasus's bravery in killing the chimera, however, Zeus then had the horse taken to his stables and given the task of carrying his lightning bolts around the world. Finally, after Pegasus's death, Zeus created a constellation of stars in the northern sky to commemorate him.

Looking into the Stars

There is actually a constellation now located in the northern sky that features as part of the unicorn story. The stars were first observed by a Dutch mapmaker named Petrus Plancius in 1612. He was creating a celestial map of the heavens, expanding on the work of the Egyptian astronomer Ptolemy of the second century CE. Plancius named the new constellations that he discovered after various animals, with one being called Monoceros Unicornis—the unicorn constellation.

This constellation consists of a relatively faint array of stars and is best viewed using a telescope, its location being most easily discerned during the early part of the year. It is located on the celestial equator, and its outline forms what resembles a dot-to-dot image of a horse-like unicorn in the sky. Monoceros Unicornis is close to the so-called "dog stars," which form the constellations of Canis Major and Canis Minor.

Back in 2002, one of the stars in the Monoceros Unicornis constellation burst into life and temporarily became the brightest star in the whole of the

Milky Way galaxy, which includes our solar system. Thanks to NASA's Hubble Space Telescope, astronomers discovered that an explosion on the surface of the star had lit up the dust surrounding it, creating an effect known as a light echo, which explained its sudden brightness.

The Lives of Unicorns

Unicorns are popularly believed to inhabit enchanted forests, living well away from people, although they may choose to reveal themselves to maidens walking through the woodland. They rest lying on the mossy ground like a horse and are believed to feed on forest fruits and vegetation. They are said to prefer areas where there are streams or larger ponds.

Several unicorns may sometimes live together, forming small herds called "blessings." Older unicorns will help to look after the young, which are known as "sparkles," because at this early age, they have a seven-pointed star on their forehead, where their horn will ultimately develop. This link with the stars is also reflected in the heavens (see page 19). It is said to take a year for the horn of a baby unicorn to grow to its maximum size.

According to a version of *Physiologus*, unicorns helped to ensure the safety of other animals living alongside them. Deadly snakes might spit their venom into lakes, causing any animal drinking there to die immediately. Only after a unicorn had waded into the lake and dipped its horn into the water, neutralizing the effects of the venom, would it be safe for the other animals to drink there. This was confirmed by Father Johann van Hesse, writing in 1389, who stated that he had seen a unicorn behaving in this way, entering the water as the sun rose.

Unicorn Magic

Perhaps unsurprisingly, a unicorn's horn was believed to have similar magical properties that could protect people from poisoning, as well as from animals, and this led to great demand for what was an exceedingly rare item. If a piece of horn was dipped into contaminated or poisoned water, it would then purify it and make it safe.

As a result, in the Middle Ages, rich and influential people who were likely to have enemies sought to obtain special ornate cups called hanaps. Reputedly made from unicorn horn, these were regarded as providing protection against poisoning for people who drank from them. Furthermore, there were positive health benefits ascribed to drinking from a unicorn's horn, as it was said to cure epilepsy and various other ailments.

Unicorn horn was also considered to be very valuable because it could detect poison in food. If it came into contact with anything that was not safe to consume, the horn would become hot to the touch and start to smoke—clear signs that the food would be dangerous to eat.

Increasing Demand

Trade in unicorn horn grew very significantly between the 1300s and 1600s as belief in its strong magical powers spread, causing its price to soar, driven by a dramatic increase in demand as well as a relative shortage in supply. Unsurprisingly, it became a very valuable item, which, at its peak, was estimated to have been worth more than ten times the value of gold.

It was possible to purchase small quantities of horn in the form of dust or small chips from apothecaries, and this practice continued until the eighteenth century. At the other extreme, however, one of the most stunning examples of supposed unicorn horn ever recorded was given in 807 CE to the Holy Roman Emperor Charlemagne. This particular horn measured almost 10 feet (3 m) in length. Over the course of the following centuries, further spectacular pieces were used as gifts to forge or seal political alliances.

In addition, other parts of the unicorn's body were considered to offer remarkable healing properties as well. Its liver, mixed with egg yolk, was said to protect against the highly disfiguring disease known as leprosy, which was common in medieval times. Leather derived from a unicorn's skin was greatly sought after, particularly as a way of warding off plague and fever, while wearing shoes made from unicorn leather helped to protect against any ailments of the feet and lower parts of the body.

Becoming a Unicorn Detective

Being an incredibly expensive item to purchase, with a highly lucrative trade in this item being built up, unicorn horn had to exist in some physical form. So where did it come from? As it was so precious—and easily faked, especially in powdered or chipped form, using horn, and even walrus or elephant ivory—those selling it typically had small pieces of whole horn on display. This provided a way to convince would-be buyers that it was genuine, at a time long before there were chemical tests to confirm the authenticity and purity of what they were purchasing.

The key distinguishing feature of unicorn horn was, of course, its spiral or corkscrew-like configuration. This wasn't something usually seen in the case of tusks or horns. The varied coloration that had been described by Ctesias had been overlooked, so it was generally assumed by this stage to be whitish.

Even at this stage in history, it is worth remembering that although mechanical printing had begun in 1440 in Europe, books were still very expensive, and also, many people were unable to read. Travel had not become significantly more straightforward or safer by the Middle Ages either, and there were no other means of general communication.

In this void, information did not spread quickly, and traditional beliefs remained largely unchallenged. Those who knew where unicorn horn could be found were not going to give up their secrets to outsiders in any event, although various expeditions were mounted to track down unicorns in the wild, with the hope of securing regular supplies of horn.

So where did it actually originate from? There is a clue in the area of the world where the largest and most valuable pieces were sourced. These came from Viking seafarers and traders in Scandinavia, indicating that it probably originated from an animal living in that part of the world, notably in the ocean. The study of natural history was still in its early days, however, and the creature with the horn was largely an animal of mystery. It was of course impossible to dive down into the depths and see it in its natural environment at that stage, let alone photograph it.

A True Unicorn

So what was this tusked animal that inspired and sustained the unicorn story? It was in fact the narwhal (also sometimes known as the narwhale) which is a particularly distinctive member of the whale (cetacean) group. It can be found in the seas of the far north throughout the year, with its distribution extending around the Arctic Circle from Canada via Greenland to Russia. The scientific name of this particular cetacean is *Monodon monoceros*, which means "one tooth, one horn," reflecting its unicorn-like appearance.

The name *narwhal* comes from the mottled grayish appearance of this whale, and originates from the old Norse word *nár*, which translates as

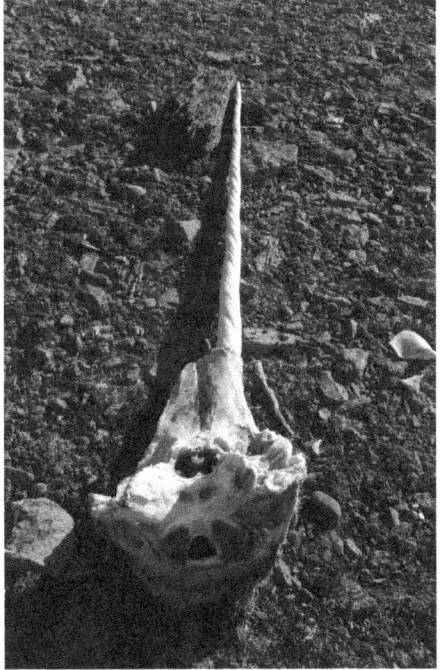

A narwhal skull with horn attached: the
source of the unicorn horn.
Photo courtesy Michelle van Dijk/
www.shutterstock.com

A living narwhal, revealing its distinctive horn.
Photo courtesy Saifullahphotographer/www.shutterstock.com

"corpse," reflecting the way in which these cetaceans float at the surface during the summer. Older males will lose this mottling, however, and can end up being pure white, bearing a closer resemblance to their near relative, the beluga whale (*Delphinapterus leucas*).

Narwhals can grow up to 18 feet (5.5 m) in length (excluding their tusk) and weigh up to about 3,500 pounds (1,590 kg). Usually, only male narwhals have a tusk, and these continue growing throughout the animal's life, which can be nearly a century in the case of males and even longer in females.

The tusk itself is formed by the greatly enlarged canine tooth in the upper jaw, on the left-hand side of the whale's mouth. It can reach more than 10 feet (3.1 m) in length and may weigh 22 pounds (10 kg). Projecting through the lip, it has a left-handed corkscrew or "helical" shape.

About fifteen out of every one hundred female narwhals also have a tusk, but this is shorter and has less of a spiraled shape, compared with that of males. On rare occasions, males may have a tusk formed by the canine tooth on the right-hand side of their mouth too. It is estimated that this applies in the case of two individuals per thousand.

There have been a number of theories advanced over the years to explain the purpose of the narwhal's tusk. It used to be thought that this was a way for males to fight and perhaps to smash a hole through the ice. As air-breathing mammals, whales need to surface regularly in order to breathe. Narwhals have also been observed by drones using their tusk to help them catch fish, but clearly this has to be an adaption, given that most females lack tusks. Recently, however, scientists have discovered that the narwhal's tusk contains literally millions of nerve endings, providing these whales with a very sensitive way of monitoring their surroundings.

Furthermore, whereas it used to be thought that when male narwhals engaged their tusks together, this was a sign of aggression (even though it was not done violently), it is now clear that such action provides a means by which these deep-diving, fish-eating whales can communicate with each other.

Narwhals face a particular danger that can sometimes result in mortality, because of their need to breathe air. As winter returns to the Arctic the openings in the sea ice can freeze over quickly. This will trap the whales so they can no longer surface, which ultimately means they will suffocate and drown. Under normal circumstances, narwhals will migrate to areas where the sea ice will not be covering the entire surface of the ocean, but groups can sometimes still get trapped and are unable to escape. After such calamities, it was possible for local people to obtain quantities of tusks, which could ultimately be sold as unicorn horn.

The Story Is Challenged

An early recorded suggestion that the narwhal was the inspiration behind tales of the unicorn and its horn was made during the reign of Queen Elizabeth I (1558–1603). She was presented with a fabulous tusk by Sir Humphrey Gilbert, who described it as coming from a "sea-unicorne." Strangely, however, this view did not become more widespread at that stage.

Gilbert's description of "sea-unicorne" for the narwhal is interesting because it used to be generally thought that every marine creature had a land-based counterpart. What didn't emerge until much later was the fact that unlike other whales, narwhals have their cervical or neck vertebrae jointed, which gives them more flexibility. In the case of other cetaceans, these bones, which form the upper part of the backbone, are fused together. Whether this is linked with the weight and length of the tusk is still unclear, but it seems likely.

In 1638, a Danish doctor and professor named Ole Worm also made the suggestion that narwhals were the source of unicorn horn and that unicorns did not exist, but his view was essentially ignored. By this stage, many influential and wealthy people had invested heavily in the unicorn myth. Worm himself died of plague in 1654, and belief in unicorns continued essentially unchanged thereafter.

Indeed, the Coronation Chair of Denmark, which was finally completed in time for the coronation of Christian V in 1671, after nine years of work, was said to have been created from the horn of unicorns. Protected by three life-size silver lions, it can be seen today at the Castle of Rosenborg, in the Danish capital of Copenhagen. The supposed unicorn horns used in the construction of this magnificent object came, of course, from narwhals, rather than unicorns.

Other Possibilities

The narwhal is a deep-diving marine mammal known by relatively few people at that stage in history. It seems almost impossible that it could be the sole source of physical evidence to justify the unicorn's existence. Furthermore, there was also the long-accepted belief extending back centuries by this stage that unicorns lived on land and were to be found in Asia.

So what are the possible terrestrial identities underpinning the appearance of a unicorn? One can be unraveled very easily, based on a detailed contemporary account. The famous Italian explorer Marco Polo, who traveled in Asia between 1271 and 1295 CE, described the unicorns that he observed there. These animals had a black horn in the center of their forehead, with their bodies being covered in dark hair. They were just slightly smaller than an elephant, with similar feet. He also noted how they enjoyed wallowing in mud and had what he reported as a very ugly appearance.

It is now clear, based on Marco Polo's account of both the appearance and lifestyle of this supposed unicorn, that he was in fact describing the Indian rhinoceros (*Rhinoceros unicornis*). Back then, it had a very much wider distribution across the Indian subcontinent than is the case nowadays. Today, unfortunately, these rhinoceroses are under serious threat of extinction, because of widespread illegal hunting for their horns.

Already Gone

There is also the possibility that a long-extinct form of rhinoceros may have helped to trigger reports of unicorns. Known as *Elasmotherium*, it lived in eastern Europe, with a range extending into Asia where unicorns were said to roam, surviving up until at least thirty-nine thousand years ago and possibly into more recent times. This meant that although these primitive rhinoceroses had definitely long disappeared before Ctesias's first account of the unicorn, their remains could easily have been found in the ground, as can still happen today. *Elasmotherium* was significantly bigger than any of today's rhinos, but what made it even more spectacular was its massive single horn, located in the center of its skull.

A Further Rarity

Another possible contributor to the unicorn story was unknown to Western scientists until 1992. This incredibly rare animal was discovered living in the Annamite Range of Vietnam's Vũ Quang National Park. Best known as the saola, it is also referred to as the spindle horn or Asian unicorn, thanks to its long, pointed horns.

There are nevertheless two horns present in living saola, rather than just one, and they can measure up to 20 inches (45 cm) in length. The saola (*Pseudoryx nghetinhensis*) is not a member of the horse family either, but is a bovid—or wild cow. It inhabits a very small area of habitat today and is critically endangered for a variety of reasons, including hunting pressure and loss of habitat. It remains unclear, though, if the saola could have played a part in the creation of the unicorn myth, given its very restricted range.

Another Identity?

A fourth terrestrial contender to have played a role in the story of the unicorn is the Arabian oryx (*Oryx leucoryx*), which is a type of antelope, again belonging to the bovid rather than the equine family. It essentially matches the unicorn in terms of color, with its body being predominantly white in the case of adult animals, although there are darker markings on the face and legs. Its horns are very long, measuring nearly 5 feet (1.5 m) in length, and ribbed, curving backward over the top of the head. They are not white in color, however, but grayish-black.

These oryxes used to roam widely throughout the Middle East, but hunting almost caused them to become extinct in the last century. Thankfully, breeding in zoos helped to provide individuals for release back to the wild, and with hunting having been banned their numbers have grown once more.

When viewed from certain angles, and especially from a distance away, the Arabian oryx appears only to have one horn, just like a unicorn. Furthermore, the myth about unicorns could also of course have come from individuals that only had one horn. Unlike deer, if an oryx loses a horn, this will not regrow again, in contrast to the antlers of deer, which are shed on an annual cycle.

A Sad Conclusion

In summary, what is clear is that the unicorn is actually a composite animal that has been created using parts of living animals molded together by various inaccurate and unchallenged descriptions in the past. Unfortunately, there is no evidence whatsoever to support the idea that it is an animal that does or indeed has ever existed, except in our imaginations.

The misplaced belief in the miraculous powers of unicorn horn has ironically nevertheless transferred across today to a surrogate of the unicorn, in the guise of the rhinoceros. This has already resulted in countless real-life casualties. Not only the Indian rhinoceros, as described by Marco Polo, but all four other living species of rhinoceros, found in parts of Africa and Asia, are under very real threat of extinction because of ruthless hunting for their horn.

Rhino horn has already become worth far more than gold, and there is now tragically the very real risk that the world's rhinos will be completely wiped out in the wild by the end of the twenty-first century. This is the result of the total myth that their horn—which simply consists of keratin, like our fingernails—actually offers magical protection and can cure our ills, as was believed to be the case with unicorn horn over the course of past centuries.

Ten Things You May Not Know About Unicorns

1   There is a National Unicorn Day in the United States each year, celebrated on April 9.

2   Unicorn tears are said to possess incredibly powerful healing properties, both for the mind and body. They are incredibly rare, however, because unicorns are believed to cry only a few times during their lifespan of several centuries, as they normally have cheerful natures. Some suggest that if a unicorn is driven to cry, it will die.

3   It is said that if a unicorn is near you in a forest but is hidden from sight, you may nevertheless detect a cinnamon smell, revealing its presence.

4   Unicorns are said to be able to help people when they are troubled by visiting them when they are asleep and dreaming, helping them to find the right path in life.

5   The link between rainbows and unicorns has only recently become prominent. This dates back to when the toy manufacturer Hasbro launched its popular *My Little Pony* series of toys in 1982 and included unicorns that had a colorful aura around their bodies.

6   The term *unicorn* is used to describe a private business startup with a value of over $1 billion. This description was first used in 2013 when there were estimated to be thirty-nine such companies trading.

7   The unicorn is the national animal of Scotland. The country also used to have two gold coins, known as the unicorn and half-unicorn, which were in circulation from 1484 until 1525 and carried the image of a unicorn.

8 There are various other unicorn-like creatures reported from other parts of the world. The rare Qilin (Chi'i-lin) is a magical, fortune-telling animal from China. First described in 2700 BCE, it has a very gentle nature but can defend itself with fire, recalling to mind a dragon. It possesses the characteristic single horn on its forehead, combined with the body of a deer and the tail of a bull.

9 There are nine mentions in the Old Testament of the Bible of the Hebrew word *re'em*, which was traditionally translated as "unicorn," although more recently, it has been interpreted as meaning "wild ox." This again reflects the confusion between these animals that has arisen in the past.

10 A patent to create unicorns was filed in 1984, although it has now expired. The idea was to transplant the horn bud in a newborn animal such as a cow or antelope, moving it to the center of the head, as in the case of a unicorn, and removing the second bud entirely. It is unclear as to whether this bizarre experiment was ever carried out.

2

MERMAIDS AND MERMEN

A typical mermaid.
Photo courtesy PeopleImages.com—
Yuri A/www.shutterstock.com

The world's oceans, even today with all the technology that we have at our disposal, still represent an area of mystery. There is much that we do not know about them, especially in terms of the different creatures that live in their depths. Imagine what it used to be like in bygone days when the continents were not mapped, and there used to be a belief that you could literally sail off the edge of the earth because it was flat. Many of the sea creatures which to us today are easily recognized were then largely unknown.

The Siren's Song

Those who set sail on overseas voyages of exploration from Europe, extending back as far as Christopher Columbus in the 1400s, reported sightings of mermaids. Belief in mermaids extends back much farther, however. The roots of the mermaid story trace back to the sirens who feature in Greek mythology. They were said to possess enchanting female-like voices, which served to draw unwary sailors into danger, luring their ships on to the rocks. As far as it is possible to tell, sirens first featured in Homer's *Odyssey*, an epic poem written in about the eighth century BCE, which traces the highly dangerous journey of the hero, King Odysseus, back to his island kingdom of Ithaca, off the west coast of Greece, after the end of the Trojan War.

Keen to hear the song of the sirens, the hero Odysseus took advice from the enchantress Circe and commanded all his crew members to plug their ears with beeswax so they could not hear the sirens' song, and to tie him to the mast of the ship. As he started to fall under their spell and begged to be released, his crew were forced to tie him tighter. Ultimately, they released him once they had sailed out of range of the sound.

Taking on a Physical Form

The sirens in Homer's poem were simply disembodied voices, and it was not until several centuries later that they gained a physical form. This occurred in another epic Greek poem called *Argonautica*, written in the early part of the third century BCE by Apollonius of Rhodes. It retells the story of Jason and the Argonauts, who set out on a journey to find the fabled golden fleece, which had come from Chrysomallos, a winged ram who had been sacrificed to the god Zeus and was regarded as a sign of kingship. Just as in the Odyssey, Jason underwent numerous tests on his journey to obtain the fleece, before returning triumphant. On this occasion, the sirens encountered by Jason were described in the story as having the bodies of women, perhaps unsurprisingly combined with those of birds, which explained their beguiling calls.

This description was mirrored by the earliest portrayals of sirens in Greek art, where they are shown as possessing the heads of women, with feathered bodies and bird-like feet. Gradually, this imagery shifted over time, with the upper body becoming human in appearance and wings being introduced too in some cases. It was also increasingly common for sirens to be portrayed with musical instruments such as lyres, which are harp-like instruments.

Up until about the fifth century BCE, sirens were shown as being either male or female, but after this period, they became exclusively female. By this stage, archaeological evidence has revealed that they had started to evolve into mermaid-like beings, described as "tritonesses." Triton was the Greek God of the Sea, who reputedly lived in a golden palace within the depths of the ocean. He was the son of Poseidon, the traditional protector of seafarers, and the sea-goddess Amphitrite.

In terms of his appearance, Triton is typically portrayed as having the upper body of a man, combined with the lower body of a fish, representing an example of what is often described as a merman. There is a different variation on this theme told by Apollonius of Rhodes, however, when Triton assisted Jason and the Argonauts back to the Mediterranean Sea after a storm had blown their ship into the Gulf of Sirte, on what is now Tunisia's eastern coast. In this telling, although Triton's father was also Poseidon, his mother was Europa (after whom the continent of Europe is named).

The Evolution of the Mermaid

A key change then followed in different editions of the *Physiologus*, an early Christian work originally published in the second century CE (see Chapter 1). At first, in this early bestiary, sirens are not only featured, but also portrayed as part woman, part bird. There was then a major transformation evident in the case of the *Bern Physiologus*, published in the first half of the ninth century, although it is believed to be a copy of an edition originally produced about four hundred years earlier.

In contrast to the text, which states that the lower part of a siren's body was avian, here for the first time was evidence of a transformation from a siren into a mermaid, as the entry was accompanied by a composite image of a woman with wings on her back and the lower part of her body being unmistakably fish-like in appearance. This marked the beginning of the end for the classical interpretation of sirens. Nevertheless, their legacy is still apparent in the English language today, with the description of "siren song" being used to describe a situation which is superficially appealing, but is destined to have a bad outcome.

The confusion continued for some time, with a Latin bestiary from the mid-1200s CE that was created in England once again including an illustration of sirens as mermaids with fish-tails, while the text persisted in saying that they were winged birds. Soon after, another bestiary showed a siren mermaid in what was to become a classic pose—holding a fish. Some bestiaries backed a more mixed approach, opting for a siren with a human upper torso, wings, and the feet of a bird, separated by the body of a fish!

Signs of Temptation

The transformation of sirens into symbols of worldly temptation had occurred in the early Christian era, and they subsequently became indistinguishable from mermaids in the medieval period. The first recorded use of the term *mermaid* is to be found in the English writer Geoffrey Chaucer's "Nun's Priest's Tale," which is one of the stories featured in *The Canterbury Tales*. This dates to approximately 1390, and the word is derived from two separate components: "mere," meaning "sea," and "maid," referring to a girl or woman. Even today, though, there is a linguistic crossover, as reflected by the French word for "mermaid," which is *sirène* or the Italian description of *sirena*.

Leonardo da Vinci (1452–1519) noted how sirens could reputedly put mariners to sleep with the beauty of their singing, allowing them to get onboard vessels and kill the crew while they slept. Strangely, as time passed it seems that some scholars, such as the Catholic teacher Athanasius Kircher (1602–1680), believed that sirens were living entities. Indeed, he highlighted the fact that they would have had their own designated area within Noah's Ark, along with all the other creatures known to live on Earth at that time in history, excluding invertebrates. He even produced calculations to show this was possible!

Beauty and Reality

By the time Christopher Columbus set sail on his epic journey in 1492 that led to the modern discovery of the New World, belief in mermaids was well established. In fact, he documented his encounter with three mermaids off the coast of the Caribbean island of Hispaniola. He noted that they were not as beautiful as they were often portrayed, having a more masculine appearance.

Beauty is a characteristic associated with mermaids going back centuries. It probably links to the idea of sirens as beautiful seductresses as well as songsters. In later bestiaries, siren mermaids (the fish version) were often portrayed holding a comb and/or a mirror, which became regarded as a symbol of vanity. They were always portrayed with long tresses that tumbled down to their shoulders.

Assuming that what Columbus and his crew encountered were not real mermaids, what could they have been? As strange as it sounds, they were almost certainly the closest living relative of elephants! Sirenians are a group of aquatic mammals found in coastal waters, estuaries, and in stretches of fresh water too. There are four living species today, with Steller's sea cow (*Hydrodamalis gigas*) having become extinct by the end of the 1700s. The sea cow had a very limited population, living in the vicinity of the Commander Islands, which lie between Russia and Alaska in the Bering Sea. They were far larger than their living relatives, growing up to a length of 30 feet (9 m), and, uniquely, could not submerge themselves completely under the waves, because of their positive buoyancy.

The belief in sightings of mermaids in the Caribbean continued long after Columbus. Edward Teach (c. 1680–1718), who was the notorious pirate better known as Blackbeard, was totally convinced of their existence. Indeed, he went so far as to avoid sailing through certain areas, which he referred to as being "enchanted," based on sightings that he and crew members had previously made in those areas. He also wrote about mermaids in his ship's log.

Much later, in the popular movie *Pirates of the Caribbean: On Stranger Tides*, released in 2011, Blackbeard (played by Ian McShane) captures a mermaid called Syrena (a role taken by Àstrid Bergès-Frisbey), reinforcing this ancient historic link.

Several reasons stemming from these sea cows or sirenians help to explain the widespread belief in mermaids. Perhaps most significantly, they are to be seen in coastal areas and are not creatures of the deep ocean. The four living species also have a wide range, being associated with all continents other than Europe. This helps to explain why such a widespread belief in mermaids developed.

With their group name of Sirenia commemorating the sirens of Greek culture, they are divided into two distinct families. Manatees form the family Trichechidae, and it was almost certainly the West Indian species (known to science as *Trichechus manatus*) with its wide distribution throughout the Caribbean region, extending as far north as Florida and south to Brazil, that Columbus and his crew encountered. The only freshwater species is the Amazonian manatee (*Trichechus inunguis*), confined to the central area of the Amazon River and its tributaries. Meanwhile, the West African manatee (*Trichechus senegalensis*) can be found in coastal waters on the opposite side of the Atlantic Ocean.

Dugongs were mistaken for mermaids.
Photo courtesy Isuruwije/www.shutterstock.com

The final member of the group, called the dugong (*Dugong dugon*), has the widest distribution of all sirenians. Its range extends along much of the east coast of Africa down to Madagascar, as well as along the western shores of India and southeast Asia down to Australia, extending farther eastward into the Pacific region. Even today, with its range having contracted significantly over recent years, the dugong is estimated to be found along coastlines that total about 87,000 miles (140,000 km) in length. It is now the sole member of its family Dugongidae, after the extinction of Steller's sea cow.

These sirenians are bigger than people, measuring 8–13 feet (2.4–4 m), but this is not apparent from a distance, the body being partly under the water. The way that the mermaid myth developed comes from the way these aquatic mammals bob around in the water when resting, with their heads clearly visible. They can adopt a vertical pose, often supporting themselves on their tail in this position, which allows them to breathe air easily through their nostrils. From a distance, their heads and upper body can look rather like those of people.

Catching a Mermaid

Investigations into this area followed when a reputed mermaid was caught in Brazil. A Danish doctor, Thomas Bartholin (1616–1680), told how it was subsequently dissected for study at Leiden University in the Netherlands. As to what state it was in by the time it arrived after a sea journey from Brazil is unclear, but this may help to explain why it had no tail. The write-up describes the remains of a "sea-man," given the scientific name of *Homo marinus*, although it is clear from the accompanying illustration that it has the appearance of a mermaid, but with short, webbed forelimbs.

Bartholin himself managed to acquire the ribs and one of the forelimbs, which became the subject of detailed illustrations. Based on the bone structure, it seems clear that this was indeed the forelimb of a manatee. He believed that the creature from which it originated was probably a type of seal, even though he did not discount its similarity to that of a person. His rationale relied on the widespread belief that land animals could have aquatic counterparts, as reflected by the case of the seahorse (*Hippocampus* species) with its distinctly equine appearance, while accepting that it was not a horse as such. A mermaid could therefore look like a person, without actually being human as such, in Bartholin's view.

More Sightings

Interestingly, during this period, other sailors reported sightings of living mermaids. The navigator and explorer Henry Hudson, who subsequently disappeared in 1611 while seeking the fabled Northwest Passage, a sea route between the Arctic Circle and North America, recorded seeing a mermaid to the north of Norway three years earlier. Then, in a similar part of the world, Dutch explorer David Danell recorded the sighting of a beautiful mermaid with flowing hair near Greenland, which eluded attempts to capture it. These sightings could not have been explained by encounters with a sirenian, and they probably relate to seals or possibly even a polar bear swimming in the sea in the case of Danell's report.

The Case of the Ambon Mermaid

Just over a century later, at some stage between 1706 and 1712, although the precise date has been lost, the remarkable capture of a living mermaid was recorded in the Moluccan Islands, which back then were under Dutch rule, although today they are Indonesian. Called the Ambon Mermaid, after the province of that name, it was reputedly caught off the island of Buru, which now forms part of the Indonesian province of Maluku.

The mermaid passed into the care of a former soldier of the Dutch East India Company, who became an associate curate of the Dutch reformed church. Samuel Fallours kept the creature in a tank of sea water, where it lived for four days and seven hours. During this period, it refused food, and the only sounds that it made were described as being like the high-pitched calls of a mouse.

Fallours created a color painting of the Amboina mermaid while it was still alive. It shows a bare-breasted, long-haired female figure down to the waist, but unlike the typical image of a mermaid, it had a long tail that was more than twice the length of the body itself. There are fins of seemingly even length and height both above and below this unmistakably piscine part of the body, with the tail being forked at its tip. A rather strange frill extending around the body is apparent where the humanoid form merges into the features of a fish. In total length it measured 5 feet (152 cm).

Based on the locality where it originated, various naturalists of the period, such as Georg Eberhard Rumphius (1627–1702) (who also worked for the Dutch East India Company), believed that the creature must have been a dugong, although he did not have the opportunity to examine it. Rather strangely, however, when an illustration of the supposed mermaid was published in 1719, in a book about the marine life of the region written by Louis Renard, a dugong was also included, but it was portrayed in a very different way. It seems unlikely that both would have appeared under separate entries if they were the same creature.

Looked at through modern eyes, the Amboina mermaid has a distinctively eel-like appearance, and there are a number of eels from that part of the world, which may account for this. It has also been suggested that a young oarfish may explain its identity. There are three known species in this case, with the largest being the giant oarfish (*Regalecus glesne*) which can attain a length of 26 feet (8 m), making it the longest of all bony fish.

Solitary by nature and rarely seen, often lurking down in the depths of the ocean, oarfish generally only surface when sick. This may explain why the Ambon mermaid seemed to be lethargic and died quite soon after being caught. The face of these fish could conceivably be mistaken for that of a person, and the greatly elongated dorsal fin rays over the head form what could be suggestive of long, trailing hair.

Eels at this stage in history would have been more commonly known, especially to Europeans, whereas the giant oarfish was not formally recognized by science until 1772. Even so, whether oarfish or eel, there is quite a bit of artistic license evident in Fallours's artwork, not least in terms of the Amboina mermaid's forked tail. It is unclear as to what happened to its remains, but they have presumably long since disappeared.

Contemporary Sightings

Almost as a postscript, it may seem strange, but there are still sightings of mermaids being made! In 1998, a diver and videographer named Jeff Leicher was on a boat about twenty minutes from Kaiwa Point, near Kona on the island of Hawai'i. He recorded how what appeared to be a beautiful woman with long, flowing hair leapt out of the water twice, about 10 feet (3 m) from the port side of his vessel, revealing that the lower part of her body was covered in fish-like scales and tapered to a large tail. She was swimming with a pod of dolphins. There were ten people on the boat who all witnessed this occurrence.

Subsequently, Leicher jumped into the water, although he had little hope of seeing the mermaid again. Yet remarkably, about an hour afterward, the mermaid touched him in the water, while he was swimming. He managed to take some photographs before she disappeared. They were subsequently submitted to a trio of reputable photo laboratories, all of whom stated that the image was real and had not been doctored in any way that they could detect.

Another multiple sighting, this time with a film crew on the alert, occurred on the Kiryat Yam beach in northern Israel. The presence of a mermaid in this area had been reported, and a documentary team from the NBC network spent an entire week on the beach, around the clock, filming both on the shore and in the water. They obtained footage of a figure diving after dark, and although team members attempted to pursue it to get a closer view, this proved to be impossible. Subsequent analysis of the footage carried out by Michael Shacht, the director of the Center for Coastal Ocean Research in Los Angeles, who examined all the evidence, concluded that although it was impossible to state that a mermaid was pictured, it was not beyond the bounds of possibility.

The footage generated a lot of interest and significantly raised the international profile of the city. It has led to the municipality offering a prize of $1 million for any proof of the existence of a mermaid in the area, which still remains unclaimed! The problem these days, of course, is that it is quite feasible to create a very convincing artificial mermaid. Indeed, this was shown by the television film called *Mermaids: The New Evidence*, first broadcast in 2013. It featured footage of supposed mermaids swimming in the Greenland Sea and gave the Animal Planet channel a record audience of 3.6 million viewers, many of whom assumed it was true, having missed the disclaimer at the end stating that it was a "science fiction" film, based on "scientific theory." It was a follow-up to *Mermaids: The Body Found*, screened the previous year, in which the purported scientists taking part were all actors. This type of program has since become known as a mockumentary.

There was some scientific basis to this hoax, however, as it drew on an explanation of mermaids first put forward thousands of years ago by the Greek philosopher Anaximander (c. 610–c. 546 BCE), who lived near what is now Balat in Turkey. He proposed the theory that humans developed from an aquatic animal ancestor citing as evidence the way children took so long to attain maturity. This was of course long before the key fossil finds in East Africa that pointed the way to this area being regarded as the cradle for humanity, where the earliest humans developed.

Today, the Aquatic Ape Theory, as Anaximander's proposal has become known, is essentially discounted by anthropologists, although there are still those who suggest that humans descended from a branch of apes that sought food on the shore, wading into the shallows, which explains our bipedal mode of locomotion today, while our brain development supposedly benefited from the regular consumption of omega-3 fatty acids that are to be found naturally in sea foods. Our relative lack of body hair, too, compared with other apes, would also have been advantageous for an aquatic lifestyle, according to proponents of the Aquatic Ape Theory.

Sea Folk

There is no doubt, however, that some groups of people have developed the ability to have a much more aquatic lifestyle than average. In Japan, the *ama* (a word that literally means "sea women") still continue a tradition that may extend back over two thousand years. In the early days, these divers sought out both seafood and abalone (*Haliotis* species) a marine mollusk with a stunning iridescent inner shell that was used to create shrines and was incorporated into gifts for the country's imperial emperors. More recently, they have used their skills to obtain pearls.

In 1893, Japanese entrepreneur Mikimoto Kōkichi discovered how to produce cultured pearls, utilizing a small island called Ojima, located in Ice Bay, Okinawa. He purchased the island from the town of Toba in 1929 and developed it for commercial pearl production, relying on the *ama* to retrieve oysters with pearls for him in the surrounding waters. In 1951, he renamed the island as Mikimoto Pearl Island, and it has subsequently become a tourist center with a museum housing a remarkable collection of items from around the world featuring pearls.

The *ama* still display their diving skills here today. The majority of *ama* throughout history have been female because they can hold their breath for longer underwater. Young girls could be trained for this role from the age of twelve by an experienced diver and often continued working through their seventies, in spite of the bitterly cold water and the depths at which they operated.

For many years, they wore traditional white clothing, which was thought to give them some protection from shark attacks, along with a distinctive headscarf. *Ama* still have a particularly distinctive way of diving, emitting a protracted whistle, expelling the air from their lungs once they surface. In the past, there were probably as many as six thousand active *ama*, but today, this tradition is upheld by fewer than a hundred.

Nor is this the only area in Asia where there is a long-standing tradition of female divers, which may have contributed to the mermaid story. In the South Korean province of Jeju, the *haenyeo* have been harvesting the fruits of the sea, in terms of conches, oysters, seaweed, and octopuses since at least 434 CE. Interestingly in this case, men took the lead role up until the 1600s, but in little more than a century, women subsequently assumed this role. This may have been because they had more subcutaneous fat under the skin, affording them better insulation in the bitterly cold waters.

In winter, *haenyeo* could remain submerged for about an hour. They then warmed up by a fire for three or four hours, before diving again for a similar period. In summer however, they could dive for as long as three hours at a time, always stashing their catches in floating nets. The advent of wetsuits has doubled the period that they can work to up to six hours throughout the year.

After seven years of training, starting around eleven years of age, a young *haenyeo* can dive to depths of 66 feet (20 m) and will be able to stay submerged for as long as three minutes at a time, before having to resurface for air. Haenyeo may continue diving regularly into their eighties. The tradition today, however, just as with the *amas*, is dying out, but various attempts have been made to preserve this way of life, with the South Korean government providing incentives to maintain the lifestyle. It has also been added to UNESCO's Intangible Cultural Heritage list, which serves to highlight and preserve unique aspects of culture around the world.

Given the long history, dating back many centuries, that surrounds these communities in Japan and South Korea, it is quite easy to envisage a situation where reports of these remarkable female divers could have morphed in the telling into the idea that they represented a female aquatic race, reinforcing the idea of mermaids in popular culture.

There are a number of tribes, stretching across an area from Indonesia to the Philippines, who have adopted a largely maritime existence. They are collectively referred to as the Samu-Bajau, or Sea Nomads, and have been living their traditional lifestyle for more than a millennium. Study of their physiology has revealed that they have undergone a variety of adaptations throughout this period.

Their spleens, which act as a reserve of oxygen-rich blood, are 50 percent larger than their land-based relatives, and this allows them to remain submerged at depth for longer than would otherwise be possible. Circulatory changes plus greater resistance to lack of oxygen, known as hypoxia, have also been detected in the population. Members of a separate Thai group of sea people, known as the Moken, have also been shown to have the ability to see much better underwater than usual, because their eyes have adapted for this purpose.

There are various descriptions of supposed "women-fish," variously known as *peche mujer* in Spanish or *anthropomorphus* in Dutch, that could have become intertwined between real people and animals. Described from the seas around the Visayan Islands in the southern-central parts of the Philippines, these accounts date back to the 1600s. There are various contemporary woodcuts revealing them to have had a very human-like appearance, but with the tails of fish. Native people used the term *duyon* for this form of mermaid, however, which in turn suggests they could have been dugongs.

Freshwater Encounters

Although most reports of mermaids are from marine environments, there are some from freshwater localities around the world. In fact, British folklore tells how the Laird of Lorntie was riding back through the old Scottish county of Forfarshire (now called Angus) when he heard the calls of what he mistook for a drowning woman in a lake near his home, only to be stopped by his servant, who realized that it was a mermaid, which would have killed him.

Scottish folklore also refers specifically to the *ceasg*, which can be encountered in both rivers and streams. She is similar to a mermaid in appearance, with the upper body of a woman, combined with the tail of a grilse or young salmon. A *ceasg* is said to grant three wishes to a person who catches her while also, it was not unknown for them to marry people. When the marriage ends, the *ceasg* will nevertheless continue watching over her descendants, bringing them good fortune by protecting them from storms, for example, should they be out at sea.

In Germany, the Lorelei Rock, towering 433 feet (132 m) above the River Rhine has gained a notorious reputation among those passing through the area on boats. As early as the tenth century CE, this stretch of the river was regarded as a site for disasters. Its actual name translates from Old German, and means "murmuring rock," and in fact, there used to be a distinctive sound that was audible when passing that point in the river. This was thought to result from the noise created by a combination of the currents and a small waterfall, which was amplified by the rock itself.

It was suggested that this was the call of a siren luring unwary boat captains onto the rock. The idea was developed by the German poet Harry Heine (1797–1856) in his famous work entitled *Die Lorelei*, telling of a beautiful female who sits combing her long golden hair on the top of the rock, distracting those traveling on the river below, resulting in their vessels being wrecked. The story captured the public imagination and was first set to music in 1837 by Friedrich Silcher (1789–1860) and then by the Hungarian composer Franz Liszt (1811–1886) and other later composers.

Today, the distinctive sound of the Lorelei rock is hard to hear, having been masked by changes in the river's topography, including the elimination of the waterfall, plus increased development in the area. Even so, accidents still happen on this feared stretch of river. In fact, the Rhine was blocked in this region as recently as 2011, following the capsizing of a barge that was carrying a cargo of 2,400 tons of potentially deadly sulfuric acid.

The Situation in Africa

The following year, in the landlocked, southern African country of Zimbabwe, dam engineers working close to the small town of Gokwe in the north of the country were attempting to make sure that pipes powered by a pump worked effectively, providing water for agricultural purposes. It emerged that there was a blockage, and local divers were sent down to investigate the cause of the problem. They quickly resurfaced, claiming to have seen a mermaid in the water, and refused to undertake any further work.

Unperturbed, the government hired a new set of divers from elsewhere in the country, but they came up from the depths and told exactly the same story. Farmers in the area also believed the water to be inhabited by mermaids. It is hard to explain what so many people would have seen, unless the water is home to unknown large fish, which, when observed in their natural habitat, look rather like mermaids. Alternatively, there could be strong currents and eddies, which are disorientating, according to a Zimbabwean government minister. There is a strong belief in mermaids in the country, however, which are regarded as possessing malevolent powers.

It took five years to address this particular case, which was finally resolved when local healers carried out a sacrifice of cattle, as well as brewing special beer, enabling them to placate the water spirits. A similar problem afflicted the Osborne Dam as well, close to the town of Mutare in the east of the country.

A Captive Audience

There is also the possibility of deliberate hoaxes, with one of the best-known cases of this type involving the sighting of a supposed mermaid recorded by passengers traveling on a ferry in 1967 close to Vancouver Island in British

Columbia. They described how she was sitting on the shore in this inaccessible spot eating from what appeared to be a whole salmon. Even today, the truth behind this sighting is not well known.

Back then, Judy Allred was working double shifts, first during the day at a doctor's office and then switching to an evening job at the Old Forge nightclub. She had met a personable pharmaceutical company representative named Andy Lord, who came up with the idea for the hoax. He thought the publicity would help to attract entries for a fishing contest.

Andy persuaded Judy to take on the persona of a mermaid, wearing a costume that he and his wife Lois had made, topped off with a long blonde wig. She changed by the small boat, being unable to walk in the costume, and was lifted into the boat along with a salmon that looked as though it was partly eaten.

She was carried to the spot on the beach at Helen Point, Mayne Island, and waited there for a pair of ferries to pass, so the chances were that she would be clearly seen by some of the passengers. But disaster nearly struck, because trapped in her costume, Judy was almost swept into the sea by the power of the wake of the passing boats. Luckily, this did not happen, and she was picked up safely in due course. Ironically, an eyewitness observed how she apparently liked the wave washing over her as she sat on the beach. There were several other local people involved in the hoax, notably a reporter called Derek Rhind, who worked on the local *Daily Colonist* newspaper, which gave generous coverage to the story, as well as a pilot who took some aerial photographs to justify the story.

Different Variations

Even in the case of mass sightings where there have been multiple witnesses, quite apart from many cases involving individual sightings of mermaids, it can be almost impossible to come up with a rational explanation—other than regarding it as a hoax, in the absence of any tangible evidence. Yet in the case of repeated encounters that took place around Indonesia's Kai Islands in 1943 during the Second World War, it may be possible to reach a different tentative conclusion. The invading Japanese troops saw creatures that the local people called "orang ikon"—translating as "man-fish" or "mermaids."

A particularly notable sighting occurred when a group of soldiers was resting by a lagoon. Their attention was drawn to a number of these so-called "mermaids," which started swimming around in the shallow water One leaped out onto a rock, emitting a strange gurgling call, while another swam in the direction of the soldiers. They responded by firing at those they could see, but the creatures escaped, seemingly unharmed. Later, the general in charge of the troops stationed on the islands also saw these strange animals at firsthand.

One of the group, a Sergeant Taro, asked the islanders to let him know if they ever captured an orang ikan. After the war ended, still fascinated by what he had seen, Taro attempted to raise some interest among the scientific community with the hope of investigating these creatures, but he failed to do so.

Based on contemporary descriptions, the orang ikon was said to be roughly 4.75 feet (1.45 m) in length, with a face and limbs resembling that of a person, plus long arms and a mouth likened to that of a carp. The skin was pinkish, with the tail being divided into two fins. Taking into account both its behavior and its appearance, a possible explanation could be that the orang ikon is a type of fish known as a mudskipper.

These unusual amphibious fish represent a branch of the goby family (Oxudercidae), with twenty-three species currently known to science. Their fins look similar to limbs and function in a similar way, which allows these fish both to jump and also crawl on land, and their facial appearance could be likened to that of a person. They can also breathe out of water, and in 2011, it was discovered that mudskippers can call to each other, but how they vocalize is still a mystery.

So although mudskippers tick a number of boxes, in terms of explaining the identity of the orang ikon, there is one clearly discernible flaw. Where the theory falls down is in terms of their size, as the orang ikon is significantly bigger than any currently known species of mudskipper. The largest on record only grows up to a maximum length of about 1 foot (30 cm). Nevertheless, the length of the orang ikon could easily have been exaggerated to some extent, as neither Sergeant Taro nor any of his comrades actually caught and measured one.

Furthermore, bearing in mind their distribution on the isolated Kai Islands, it is quite feasible that these mysterious aquatic creatures could turn out to be an unknown species of mudskipper. Clearly, they were well known to the locals and the mystery could still be solvable, even after more than eight decades.

The Evidence of a Mermaid's Tears

There is a story from many years ago about how there was a mermaid who fell in love with the handsome captain of a sailing ship. She tried to watch over him, keeping his ship away from the rocks, using the siren sound of her voice. But she realized that they could never be together, with their worlds being so different.

Nevertheless, she made the god Poseidon jealous of her love for the man, and he stirred up a huge storm that threatened to swamp and sink the captain's ship. The man battled desperately to keep the ship upright, but ultimately he found himself swept overboard Moments from drowning, he was rescued by the mermaid, who managed to grab him, keeping his head above the water.

She called out, singing without words, and the sound of her voice miraculously calmed the storm. The crew were then able to rescue the captain who kept saying in a state of apparent delirium that he had been rescued by a mermaid, although she was no longer to be seen.

Poseidon, enraged that she had used magic, which was his preserve, to save her love, condemned her to live in darkness at the bottom of the ocean. She cried large tears that were colored like the shimmering appearance of her tail. Fish who felt sorry for the mermaid's plight resolved to carry her tears into the shallows so they could be washed up on to the shore, in the hope that the captain might see them and think of her.

Even today, if you walk along a beach, there is a chance that you will find her tears there on the shoreline, although you will likely have little or no idea as to how old they are. Fragments of glass have washed up on beaches probably over the course of some four thousand years, matching the length of time that glass-making has been carried out.

Broken glass could be thrown or tipped deliberately into the ocean, in the same way that glass vessels would have vanished beneath the waves when a ship sank. This marks the start of its transformation into a mermaid's tears—better known as sea glass, which has a distinctive appearance. As the glass is moved along on ocean currents, rubbing on rocks and pebbles, its sharp, broken edges will become smoothed off, and over time, thanks again to abrasion from the sand and gravel, as well as the relative acidity of sea water, it becomes cloudy rather than clear, developing a frosty appearance.

So-called "pirate" glass is not always easy to spot, being black in appearance and only showing its true dark olive green color when held up to the light. Light green and brown glass are most common, with blue, purple, and particularly pink being found far less frequently, while clear glass has become more common over recent years.

There are actually a number of so-called Glass Beaches, of which the best known is located next to the MacKerricher State Park, adjacent to the city of Fort Bragg in California. This was formed from the city's dump site, when all the trash was simply thrown into the ocean in three designated spots near the city, from 1906 up until 1967. The glass ended up being broken into small pieces over the course of the decades, forming a beach that has subsequently become a tourist attraction. There is another similar glass beach at Benicia, also in California, and a third at 'Ele'ele, which is an industrial area near Port Allen Harbor in Hawai'i, where many pieces have washed up, but the covering there is less spectacular.

Meeting Popular Demand

People were fascinated by tales of mermaids, and were keen to see evidence that they actually existed. In true entrepreneurial spirit, there were many during the nineteenth century in particular who were keen to supply such proof, with little worry about the veracity of their claims. Their aim instead was to make a fortune from the gullible, as the case of the Feejee mermaid reveals.

The story begins in 1822, with an American ship captain named Samuel Barrett Edes. He paid the eyewatering sum of $6,000 for the Feejee mermaid (roughly equivalent to $160,000 today), borrowing this money from the expense account of his ship to fund the purchase. At this stage, it appears that the origins of the creature were unknown, but it provided an example of the skills of Japanese fishermen, who had carefully combined the upper body of a blue-faced monkey with the rear half of a salmon.

The truth subsequently emerged, based on the experience of a Dutchman named J. F. van Overmeer Fisscher, who was living on the trading outpost of Dejima. This was an artificial island connecting to the port of Nagasaki, which represented the only part of Japan that was open to Westerners during the Edo period of isolation, extending from 1600 to 1869. Those who were lucky enough to discover that artificial mermaids could be purchased relatively cheaply there were able to resell them for a fortune in Europe. J. F. van Overmeer Fisscher was offered a wide range of other options, including twin-headed dragons, ultimately taking some examples back with him to his home at The Hague in the Netherlands.

But just as fortunes could be made, they could also be lost, and unfortunately Captain Edes's naivety cost him dearly. He returned to London, and placed his so-called "mermaid" on display at the Turf Coffee House in St. James's Street in the center of the city but he never recouped his massive outlay on it.

America's Greatest Showman Gets Involved

After his death, his son sold the figure in 1842 to Moses Kimball (1809–1895), who ran the Boston Museum. Intrigued but uncertain about this new exhibit, he in turn arranged to show it to the great American showman, P. T. Barnum, taking it to New York City in the summer of that year.

Barnum in turn sought advice from a naturalist, hoping that he would authenticate it as being genuine, but his expert demurred from so doing. In typical style, though, Barnum saw an opportunity to make a profit. Rather than purchasing the piece, given the uncertainty surrounding its true identity, he agreed to lease it for display at a fee of $12.50 (approximately $470 today), leaving Kimball as its official owner, and immediately launched a publicity campaign around what was henceforth to be known as the Fejee or Fiji Mermaid.

An associate of Barnum's, called Levi Lyman wrote to New York newspapers from various locations in the United States, with the aim of generating interest in the exhibit. He also constructed the false identity of Dr. J. Griffin, who was purportedly an Englishman, and said to be a member of the British Lyceum of Natural History (even though no such body existed). It was claimed that Griffin had acquired the mermaid in the South Pacific, with the thought that it may have originated from the island of Fiji.

Building on the story, Lyman, playing the role of Griffin, then checked into a hotel in Philadelphia. He was only too willing to allow privileged viewings to the owner and the press who descended on the building, reinforcing the validity of the story and increasing media interest.

Knowing that reports would have filtered back to New York, P. T. Barnum himself now became involved. He toured the newspaper offices explaining how he had attempted to persuade Griffin to bring the creature to New York, and place it on display for a period at his museum, but he had been unsuccessful. Strangely, he had prepared a woodcut portraying an archetypal beautiful mermaid, which he was intending to use to promote the exhibition, but under the circumstances, it was now of no value—though he thought the newspapers might like to have it, in case they wanted to run something about the story. They duly obliged! In addition, Barnum had also had 10,000 leaflets printed, showing a similar image, which he had distributed around the city.

Excitement grew to a fever pitch, and the stage was set for a triumphant exhibition, once Griffin finally relented and agreed to put "his" mermaid on show for a week at the Concert Hall on New York's Broadway. People flocked to see it, and subsequently, Griffin generously accepted Barnum's invitation to place it on display for a month at his American Museum. He was also persuaded to give lectures to some of the visitors about this remarkable find.

Those who paid to see the specimen saw an unattractive dark and rather monstrous creature. It was as far removed from the beautiful popular imagery of a mermaid that Barnum had used to promote the event as it was possible to be, but there appear to have been few complaints.

Indeed, after its time in New York, the Fiji Mermaid then traveled south, but this tour did not go as well, and had to be cut short when it reached Charleston's

Masonic Hall in South Carolina. The two newspapers in the area were lined up on opposite sides of the debate about the authenticity of the specimen. The discussion became heated, and Alanson Taylor, who was both Barnum's uncle and manager of the exhibition, decided to cut the exhibition short, so as to prevent the Fiji Mermaid being attacked and destroyed by its opponents. He claimed that it was too fragile to be dissected and undergo further scientific investigation, while loudly criticizing those who dared to doubt its authenticity.

It then appears that the Fiji Mermaid traveled between Barnum's museum in New York, and that of Moses Kimball in Boston. It was also exhibited for a brief period back in London in 1859. After this, the whereabouts of the Fiji Mermaid became rather murky. It was said that the mermaid was destroyed by a fire that swept through Barnum's American Museum in 1865, although the evidence suggests it was in Boston at that stage. It could have been destroyed there in another blaze in the early 1880s. Alternatively, there is the possibility that it could have survived, and passed into the care of the Peabody Museum of Archaeology and Ethnology at Harvard. It is unclear if the specimen in the collection there today is the same one, partly because there are no photographs of the original purchased by Kimball. Certainly, it was not unique—various other similar composite creatures were made in Asia, and some are now present in museum collections elsewhere.

A Merman Surfaces

An equally bizarre tale emerged as the result of an unplanned visit to the Banff Indian Trader Store by Ken Jeremiah. He walked into the store and was confronted by what he was told was a merman that had supposedly lived in nearby Lake Superior. There was an accompanying article said to date from 1824, quoting a Stoney Nakoda Indian named Enoch Baptiste, to justify the claim that this strange creature had come from the lake, leaving this stretch of fresh water cursed.

However, the truth of the matter is somewhat different, as Ken Jeremiah discovered. Norman Luxton was a newspaper man who worked for various papers. He became friendly with an individual named John Voss, who had the crazy idea of circumnavigating the world in a native Nootka canoe, which was already a century old by that stage. The pair set off from British Columbia and paddled across the Pacific, traveling some 10,000 miles (16,000 km) in five months before disaster struck. The canoe collided with a reef off the coast of Fiji, causing the trip to be abandoned. Luxton came back to Banff, to recover from his injuries and launched various businesses, including the Trader Store. A number of his items subsequently passed to the Whyte Museum, and included in the paperwork is a shipping receipt for an item described as a "fish man," which had been sent to him from Java.

It seems likely that they could have reached this part of the world before the trip had to be abandoned, and so Luxton could clearly have made the purchase. Given his way with words, it is also quite likely that he subsequently concocted and publicized the story, adding the native Indian link to it. Given that his store sold associated items, this story would have provided very useful publicity: a view echoed to Jeremiah by the current owner of the Trading Post, who had actually known Norman Luxton.

As for the supposed merman today, it looks rather tired. Traces of gray hair are evident on the head and other parts of its upper body. The bottom half is clearly piscine in origin, although it is impossible to guess the type of fish used.

Medical Involvement

There is a possibility that a human medical condition could have reinforced the belief that mermaids were real. Taking the name of the siren, this condition, called sirenomelia and also known as mermaid syndrome, results in babies being born with fused legs, causing the lower part of their body to look rather like the tail of a mermaid. It is a very rare condition, with an incidence of approximately one case per one hundred thousand births on average, and is accompanied by fatal changes to the internal body organs, affecting the urogenital and gastrointestinal tracts.

Strangely perhaps, it does not appear to have been documented prior to the publication of a medical tome entitled *Human Monstrosities* in 1891, although almost inevitably, cases would have occurred before then.

Most recently, a supposed mummified mermaid, reputedly caught off the Japanese island of Shikoku sometime between 1736 and 1741, has been subject to intense scientific investigation. It is a relatively small example, measuring only one foot (30 cm) in height. This specimen was kept in a shrine in the Enjuin Temple, at the city of Asakuchi, and reputedly, anyone who consumed its body was guaranteed eternal life. Tests carried out by the Kurashiki University of Science and the Arts have, however, now revealed that there was no skeleton present. Its jaws, teeth, and fins were derived from fish, while the hair on its head was mammalian. Otherwise, it was totally artificial, being created from pieces of paper and cloth, and is thought to have been made in the late 1800s.

The island nation of Japan has a long tradition of folklore concerning aquatic creatures. The ningyo is similar to that of a mermaid, but is generally regarded as less attractive. It is often being portrayed as having the head of a monkey, along with the teeth of fish, while its body is covered in golden scales, although its appearance can be very variable. Initially, back in the seventh century CE, the ningyo (which literally means "human fish") was regarded as living in fresh water. Sometimes, it has the head of a reptile combined with the body of a fish. Another variant, called the amabie or amabiko, has a beak corresponding to that of a bird, and is credited with the ability to foretell the future. In common with other mermaid tales, it is popularly believed that the ningyo produces tears that consist of pearls.

As in the case of the ningyo from the Enjuin Temple, there is a widely-held belief that eating its flesh will lead to great longevity or even eternal life. A well-known Japanese story tells how a fisherman served a meal of a ningyo to his friends, but they declined to eat it, and then his young daughter unwittingly ate the creature. She is said to have become a nun, and subsequently lived for eight hundred years.

Such is the level of interest in mermaids that in some parts of the United States, there are mermaid shows. The most famous of these is performed within the Weeki Wachee Springs State Park lying north of Tampa in Florida, with the four hundred seat auditorium submerged to give an excellent view to the audience. This venue was first established by stunt swimmer and entrepreneur Newton Perry, opening in 1947, before becoming a state park in 2008. The caves under the freshwater springs here are now believed to be the deepest yet discovered in the United States, extending down to a depth of over 400 feet (122 m). Various productions about merfolk have been shot at the springs, including *MerPeople*, a four-part documentary series commissioned by Netflix that aired in 2023. The series investigated the field of "mermaiding" and the leading performers involved.

In conclusion, there is actually a recent incontrovertible record of a mermaid saving the life of a diver, off the coast of Catalina Island, California. In 2022, Elle Jimenez encountered an unconscious diver who was foaming at the mouth, and thanks to her diving training as a participant in mermaid shows, she was able to assist him and get him emergency treatment, so he survived.

Ten Things You May Not Know About Merfolk

1   The activity now described as "mermaiding" has become a popular pastime within the fantasy cosplay realm, from its early beginnings about 2004. Special costumes are available with a mono fin attached to the feet that creates an effective representation of a mermaid's fish-like tail.

2   In 2020, mermaiding then became recognized as a sport. The body wave movement down through the tail is a central part of the routine at events such as the World Mermaid Championship, and is described as the dolphin kick.

3   Mermaid fandoms have also become popular over recent years.

4   The most famous story about merfolk is *The Little Mermaid,* a fairytale written by the Danish writer Hans Christen Anderson, which was first published in 1837.

5   The story led to what is now a world-famous bronze statue of a mermaid resting on a rock created by sculptor Edvard Eriksen in 1913, which can be seen on the waterfront in Langelinie Park, Copenhagen.

6   One of the most popular mermaid films of recent years has been Disney's animated musical version of Anderson's fairytale, released

in 1989. *Splash*, starring Daryl Hannah as a mermaid alongside Tom Hanks is probably the most popular mermaid-themed film.

7 The image of the Mermaid of Warsaw, which appears on the coat of arms of this Polish city, dates back in various forms to 1390. It is said that a mermaid was releasing fish from fishermen's nets in the area. They spotted her, and became enchanted by her song. Subsequently a wealthy merchant managed to trap the mermaid, and hearing her distress, some of the fishermen rescued her. Since then, the mermaid has sought to protect the city.

8 In Scandinavian culture, sightings of mermaids are believed to be linked to storms.

9 According to Brazilian folklore, the *para* or *mãe-d'agua* (literally meaning "mother of the water") are beautiful women with long hair who would lure fishermen to their deaths in water.

10 Variations on the mermaid theme exist on every continent, reflecting the widespread global fascination of what could be concealed out of our sight in both fresh water and the sea.

3

THE WORLD OF DRAGONS

A statue on the famous dragon bridge (known local-
ly as "Zmajski most"), which crosses the Ljubljanica
River in Ljubljana, the capital of Slovenia.
Photo courtesy Matej Kastelic/www.shutterstock.com

Stories about dragons exist in many different cultures worldwide, extending back over the course of millennia, and while the appearance of dragons is varied, one thing that they all have in common is evident reptilian features. The European roots of dragon mythology seemingly trace back to the region which extends today from the eastern end of the Mediterranean across to the Caspian Sea, centered on the area that was known as Mesopotamia.

What is generally accepted as the earliest surviving portrayal of a dragon-like creature is the remarkable representations of the *mušḫuššu*, to be found on the Libation vase of Gudea, which dates back to about 2100 BCE. It appears to be very much a composite animal, although the description of *mušḫuššu* literally translates from the ancient Sumerian language as "fierce snake." Its slender body is indeed highly reminiscent of a serpent, with a forked tongue in its mouth, although it also possesses wings, as well as powerful legs, distinctive horns and a crest extending down its neck.

Subsequent portrayals of the *mušḫuššu* were incorporated into the Ishtar Gate, which was constructed within the ancient city of Babylon, being created about 569 BCE on the instructions of King Nebuchadnezzar II. By this stage, the *mušḫuššu* appears in the form of a distinctive quadruped, supporting itself on four longer legs. These display the paws of a lion on the front feet, with the talons of an eagle on the hind legs.

Combined with a narrow head and neck, maintaining the originally serpentine theme, this image is nevertheless probably more reflective overall of a monitor lizard (*Varanus* species). This group of reptiles is found in the region, and they possess a forked tongue like a snake, along with a scaly body and a long, tapering tail. The *mušḫuššu* served to symbolize Marduk, who was regarded as the god of creation and became linked with the planet Jupiter.

Confusion Reigns

One of the difficulties about interpreting dragons is their wide variability in appearance, and this makes it difficult to define them compared with other mysterious creatures. So how are they best described? They typically display some recognizable reptilian features, generally resembling snakes more closely than lizards, although their overall appearance is composite, as shown by the case of the *mušḫuššu*, which also displays avian and mammalian characteristics.

Interestingly, the ancient Greek word for dragon, which is δράκων (or *drákōn*), is the same as that sometimes used for snake, confirming this link. This overlap was subsequently reinforced by Roman writers such as Virgil, who described a fierce battle between a massive constrictor snake in the poem *Culex*, referring to the creature as "serpens," but also as "draco," meaning "dragon."

A feature of early accounts about dragons is the way that they are often described as being multi-headed. These link to the mythology surrounding battles with the Hydra, which was a greatly feared creature said to possess up to one hundred heads capable of breathing fire—a feature that also became ascribed to dragons. Greek literature contains various references to both the Hydra and similar creatures. The Greek word *hydra* actually translates as "water snake." Writing during the seventh century BCE, Hesiod describes a fire-breathing serpent called Typhon, which had one hundred snake-like heads and finally ended up being vanquished in a titanic battle with the Greek god Zeus. In other portrayals, Typhon is described more in the form of a winged dragon, rather than as a snake.

Hesiod was also the first known author to tell the tale of how Zeus's son went on to destroy the Lernaean Hydra, which was itself a descendant of Typhon. It lived close to the Greek city of Argos, in the swamps of Lerna, which were believed to mark an entrance to the underworld. The earliest representation of the Hydra comes in the form of a pair of brooch pins or fibulae, dating back to approximately 700 BCE, which show it as possessing six heads, but the number of heads varies significantly in subsequent representations. It had even gained a second tail in a portrayal dated to about 500 BCE, although textual accounts only refer to multiple heads.

Greek legend tells how Eurystheus charged Heracles (who is better known today as Hercules) to kill the Hydra, as one of his so-called Twelve Labors. As he decapitated the beast, his nephew Iolaus burnt its neck to prevent the Hydra regenerating more heads. Thus working together, they defeated the creature. Ultimately, Heracles was faced with just the central, immortal head. Using a golden sword gifted to him by the goddess Athena, legend tells how he finally was able to axe this head from the body as well.

Even in this state, however, it thrashed around fiercely on the ground, and Heracles had to be careful to avoid any contact with its toxic blood, which would have been fatal. He managed to throw it safely down into a deep cavern in the ground and then filled the hole with heavy rocks, effectively trapping its head in the chasm. Heracles then dipped his arrows in some of the spilled blood and was able to use these to kill Ladon, a huge snake that was constantly awake and guarded a golden apple present in the Garden of the Hesperides. This was one of his subsequent labors, having dispatched the Hydra.

There is actually a partially factual explanation surrounding the Hydra's death, and it involves snakes, at a time before the existence of venom was understood. Clearly there was obviously something deadly about the bites of certain snakes, and it could easily have been believed that venom as we understand it today was in fact present in the snake's blood. Furthermore, decapitating a snake can lead to a gruesome spectacle whereby its head moves around in what could be perceived as an aggressive manner, having been removed from its body. Indeed, people are even known to have sustained fatal bites from the detached head of a venomous species of snake. As for the story of many heads, perhaps this might be linked to the difficulty of catching such snakes safely, their agile movements being suggestive of them having more than one head.

A particularly famous early account of a dragon features in the story of Jason and the Golden Fleece. Jason was a Greek mythical figure, and the leader of a group called the Argonauts, who were commanded to find the mythical golden fleece originating from a winged ram named Chrysomallos. By succeeding in his task, Jason would regain the throne of Iolcus, a Greek city that lay in the area of Thessaly in the east of the country. Dating back to at least the eighth century BCE, this tale has been retold many times, in different forms.

The ram's fleece was guarded by a massive dragon reputedly bigger than a ship rowed by fifty people. Some versions of the story say that Jason killed the dragon and so was able to take the fleece. On the other hand, *Argonautica*, a poem describing the event written by Apollonius of Rhodes, indicates that Jason's female companion, Medea, managed to persuade the dragon to drink a draft of a sleeping potion, which meant that he could simply take the fleece. The Greek playwright Euripides's work called *Medea*, originally performed in 431 BCE, and the only one of a trilogy of plays to have survived, takes the story one stage further. Euripides credits Medea with slaying the dragon, and in the closing act, she flies off on a sled pulled by a pair of dragons.

Changing Perceptions

There were moves away from treating dragons purely as mythical figures in the later classical period however, transposing them into living animals. The Greek historian Herodotus (c. 484–425 BC) wrote about how huge serpents could be found in the area that is now known as western Libya. At that stage, northern Africa was a fertile agricultural area rather than the desert of today, which became known as the breadbasket of the Roman Empire.

It is therefore quite possible that Central African rock pythons (*Python sebae*) actually extended that far north in terms of their distribution during that period in history, whereas today they are only found south of the Sahara Desert. Ranking as the continent's largest snake and capable of attaining a maximum recorded length of about 20 feet (6 m), these pythons are even capable of preying on crocodiles, although they rarely attack people. They are very adaptable in terms of their habitat and will enter water readily.

A variety of different descriptions of dragons as living creatures followed, confirming a widespread belief in their existence. Philostratus, who was a Greek writer living about 200 BCE, gave a detailed description of some with tusks, likening these to the biggest examples seen in pigs, but he noted they could be distinguished by having a twisted appearance and sharp pointed tips that resembled the teeth of sharks.

Other later writers contributed to the impression that dragons were living, physical beings. Claudius Aelianus (c. 175–235 CE), often simply known today as Aelian, included them in his series of seventeen creatures grouped under the title of *De Natura Animalium* (translating as "On the Nature of Animals"). It has been suggested that these were probably based to a large extent on those of earlier authors, whose works have now been lost, with the stories being passed down through the generations. Aelian recorded how the largest dragons could be found in what is modern-day Ethiopia, in northeastern Africa. They grew to a length of 180 feet (55 m) and hunted elephants. They also apparently had a very long lifespan, rivalling that of any other known animal.

There was continuing confusion at that stage between what we interpret as a dragon today and large snakes. Like Herodotus before him, it may well have been that Aelian was again referring to the Central African rock python, which still occurs in Ethiopia today, and given the monstrous size of these snakes, it would clearly be tempting to suggest that they could prey on elephants.

Aelian also documents that during his invasion of modern-day India, Alexander the Great (356–323 BCE) encountered what was described as a massive dragon that inhabited a cave, where it was worshipped by the local people. It hissed very aggressively and had a massive head. Alexander's soldiers left it undisturbed and did not see it emerge from its lair, but it was reputedly "seventy cubits" in length, equivalent to 105 feet (32 m) in modern measurements. Its identity is unclear, but in this case, it was probably an Indian python (*Python molurus*).

The ancient Greek word δράκων or *drákōn* actually meant "giant serpent," and interestingly, this is believed to be linked to the fact that snakes always have their eyes open and cannot blink, being derived originally from the verb which translates as "to see." The Romans adopted the word *draco* in their language, which again describes a huge snake or dragon. Today, in modern zoology, the Draco is commemorated by a group of Asiatic lizards that have leathery membranes on each side of the body that serve as wings, allowing them to glide short distances.

An Asian Perspective

The image of dragons is widespread throughout Asia, just as it is in Europe. Belief in creatures of this type has a potentially even longer history on this continent too. There are images that have been interpreted as dragons found on Neolithic pottery dating back approximately ten thousand years, with other portrayals discovered on vessels used for ritual purposes from the later Bronze Age. Indeed, the power of the dragon was considered to be so strong that it is credited with creating humanity itself, according to the Miao people, whose homeland lies in southern China. A dragon there is said to have transformed monkeys that entered its cave into people by breathing on them.

Dragons were also considered to be instrumental in controlling the weather. There was a widespread belief in the ability of dragons to impact the weather and particularly the advent of rainfall. This in turn probably led to them being given wings—with this characteristic seemingly having arisen in Asia and being confined to those dragons that impacted the weather. One of the most long-standing and well-known accounts of this type concerns a black-colored dragon known as Short-tailed Old Li. He triggered immense feelings of shock after his birth to a poor couple in Shandong. His mother passed out, while his father tried to kill him, attacking him with a spade. Luckily, the young dragon escaped, but not before losing part of his tail, which helps to explain his name. He flew away a long distance, before alighting in northeast China, where he settled in the river that is internationally referred to as the Amur, although it is still better known in the country itself as Heilongjiang, which means "Black Dragon River." It is said that every year, Short-tailed Old Li commemorates the death of his mother, by returning home and bringing the rains with him.

Rain gods are traditionally very important in Chinese culture, and many of these have taken the form of dragons over the course of many centuries. Dong Zhongshu (179–104 BCE), a leading philosopher during the first period of the Han Dynasty (extending from 202 BCE to 9 CE), advised making clay figurines of dragons when there was a drought and arranging for the younger members of the community to dance among them, so as to draw the rain dragon to the region. In the later Qing dynasty (1636–1912 CE), the advice was either to throw dirty items into a pool where a dragon lived, or to use a tiger bone instead. This was because dragons were said to dislike dirty surroundings in addition to being fearful of tigers, so in either case, such actions would ensure there was heavy rain to cleanse their surroundings.

Even today, a number of Chinese traditions continue to reflect the links between dragons and the weather. Dragon boat races, for example, have been held by villages for over two thousand years, with teams competing against each other, paddling their distinctive dragon-headed boats. This was thought to ensure a good crop, although an alternative explanation has been linked to these events. It involves a poet and warrior called Qu Yuan (c. 340–278 BCE), who drowned in the Miluo River, sacrificing himself to highlight the political corruption of that era. Local people took to their boats and paddled after Qu Yuan in a forlorn attempt to save him, making as much accompanying noise as possible with their drums, in the hope of driving off the ferocious dragons that were said to lurk in the river.

In order to ensure a good harvest, villagers also made dragons that could be as long as 16 feet (4.9 m) out of materials like strips of bamboo, which provided a framework with cloth covering it. Designs of this type are said to date back to the 1200s. Such sculptures were paraded through the local area, laying the foundations of what have become recognized as dragon dances. These are still a typical feature of the celebrations surrounding the Chinese New Year and other festivals today, with the performers using poles running along its length to convey its serpentine and sinuous movements.

Many villages had their own particular variation of the dragon dance, and in total, over seven hundred forms have been recognized. The dragons portrayed differ both in their appearance and their size. One of the most distinctive is simply comprised of a chain of human dancers, which may number hundreds of people. The color of the dragon is both variable and symbolic, with green traditionally indicating hopes for a good harvest, while gold or silver suggests wealth and red is an indicator of excitement. Unfortunately, however, it is difficult to trace the development of dragons used in these dances down through the centuries, because nowadays, there are no survivors from farther back in history than 1878. Thanks to the items used to make them, these

A Chinese dragon in a parade.
Photo courtesy Alexey Fedorenko/www.shutterstock.com

ceremonial dragons were fragile, and it was also traditional to set fire to them once their working lives had ceased.

Imperial Symbols

The power of dragons to impact on the environment probably also contributed to the links between them and the emperors of China, which started during the Han Dynasty (202 BCE–9 CE/25–220 CE). Over time, dragons became imperial symbols, associated with the emperors, and during the Tang Dynasty (608–911 CE), the dragon emblem was portrayed on the emperor's robes and sometimes on those of high-ranking court officials too. Subsequently, during the Yuan dynasty (1271–1368 CE), dragons were distinguished on the basis of their number of claws, and only the emperor could use the image of the five-clawed dragon, which also had a pair of horns. Princes and the nobility were permitted to use the symbol of a dragon with four claws instead.

Perhaps the most famous form of Chinese dragon, partly because of its use in heraldry, is the Azure Dragon, also known as Quin Long. It was during the long-established Qing dynasty that this dragon was portrayed on China's national flag, from 1862 to 1912, and as was usual, there was a flaming pearl above the dragon's head, indicating wealth and prosperity, with the flag itself having a yellow background, which was a color associated with the emperor.

Although Chinese dragons traditionally did not have wings (aside from the winged dragon that impacts the weather), they were still credited with the power of flight, thanks to the presence of a prominent swelling on the head, traditionally referred to as the *chimu*, although in a few cases, they are portrayed with wings that resemble those of bats. The idea of dragons being able to fly and carry people on their back had surfaced at an early stage in history—an idea revisited repeatedly by writers in recent times. Back then, it was believed that someone tied to the back of a dragon could travel quickly over a long distance. Yet disaster was likely to await if they flew over the sea, as the dragon would rapidly lose its strength and plunge into the water.

What is interesting in the case of these dragons is that instead of being based on a mythological belief that subsequently becomes rationalized and explained through a living creature, the situation in this case seems to have been reversed. It appears that Chinese dragons evolved from portrayals of different types of living animal, which then merged into a composite creature and subsequently took on a life of its own. The Chinese scholar Wang Fu, also sometimes referred to as Jiexin (82–167 CE), who lived during the Hang Dynasty, recorded nine different animal influences that were evident in the typical dragon.

The actual head was based on that of a camel, while the horns were like those of a stag. The neck resembled that of a snake, the ears were reminiscent of those of cattle. The underparts looked like those of a clam, and the scales on the body corresponded to those of a carp. In terms of the dragon's feet, its soles reflected those of a tiger, while its claws were inspired by the talons of an eagle. Others suggested its belly was more like that of a frog, and its eyes appeared like those of a rabbit, although Wang Fu described them as being inspired by a demon. All these animals occurred within China.

It is tempting to suggest that people in different parts of China may have modified the generic dragon into local forms, incorporating parts of animals with which they were familiar. The tendrils often portrayed on the dragon's head have been linked to the sensory barbels that are present around the mouths of carp and catfish.

Dragons also evolved over time. The earliest representations of Chinese dragons, dating back to the Neolithic period, took the form of a creature with the distinctive head of a pig combined with a quite stocky, limbless body form that was known as *zhūlóng*. The body shape gradually changed, however, becoming more snake-like. Carvings of these early dragons were often included in graves, indicating that right from their earliest days, dragons probably had a ritualistic significance.

Dragons Elsewhere in Asia

The impact of Chinese dragons extended to surrounding countries too, such as Japan. They soon became integrated into Japanese culture, being described there as "ryū" or "tatsu." The earliest references to dragons in Japan can be traced back to the *Kojiki*, a work published in 680 CE, which translates as "An Account of Ancient Matters." It reflects a number of long-standing beliefs and traditions documenting older oral stories and tracing the ancestry of the ruling imperial family, called the Yamato.

The *Kojiki* includes references to several dragons, as does a subsequent book, entitled *Nihon Shoki* or *Nihongi*, which was published in 720. These so-called "Japanese Chronicles" offer a more detailed insight into the origins of ancient Japan, although again, it was written in classical Chinese (the language used for literature in Japan at that time). The names of different Japanese dragons are also reflective of their Chinese origins, as with the "Four Dragon Kings of the Seas." According to Chinese mythology, these four dragon kings possessed immense power, being able to bring rain, cause flooding, and also stop storms.

Just as in China, there was a widespread belief in the dragon's power to influence rainfall in Japan. Indeed, villagers living in Okumura, close to the town of Edo, would traditionally build a dragon using bamboo, straw and magnolia leaves, as a means of overcoming drought in their region. In general, Japanese dragons were believed to have a distinctly serpentine shape and were equipped with three rather than four or more claws on each foot. This mirrors the earliest descriptions of dragons from China, which were originally said to have three claws rather than five.

The arrival of Buddhist monks also introduced dragon legends to Japan from other parts of Asia, notably the Indian subcontinent, where a number of serpentine dragon forms are well-recognized. Different forms of the Nāga are prominent in this region and bear a distinct resemblance to serpents, although their appearance can vary significantly. The majority have no limbs, while their number of heads will vary, depending on their status. One of the best known is the so-called "Nāga King" called Apalāla, who was converted to Buddhism by the Buddha himself just prior to his death. Like a number of nāgas, Apalāla is closely linked to water.

The reptilian link is also reinforced in the case of the Mahoraga, which are related to the Nāga. Belonging to the Uragas, which are regarded as primitive reptilian beings, they are recognized in Buddhism as one of a group of eight deities, being portrayed with a partial but nevertheless variable humanoid appearance—either with the head of a snake and the body of a human, or alternatively, as having a humanoid body covered in reptilian scales. This has inspired various science fiction writers, artists, and filmmakers. The Mahoraga were believed to be giant serpents that adopted a subterranean existence. They lived on their sides and caused the earth to rotate and could occasionally trigger earthquakes.

The concept of the Nāga also took root in the guise of the Neak, also known as the Khmer dragon, in the area of what is now modern-day Cambodia in Southeast Asia, where the majority of people are Buddhist. As in the case of its Indian counterpart, it is frequently portrayed in the guise of a cobra, with a variable number of heads, which can number up to nine in the case of the highest-ranked individuals. This trait distinguishes the Neak from the Maker, which has a head that more closely resembles that of a crocodilian.

A belief exists in Tibet, a country lying between India and China, in a dragon of thunder called Druk, who is said to reside on Mount Everest. Credited with bringing snow and rain to lower levels, Druk is portrayed as having a serpentine form, resembling China's Shenlong who, it was believed, could control the weather. If Shenlong was angered, the consequences could be dire and might range from drought to flooding.

In Korea, the Yong (also sometimes known as the Mireu) is a direct counterpart of the Chinese sky dragon called the Lóng. Once again, this Korean dragon is linked with the weather, as well as water, being credited with creating rainfall.

The Reappearance of Dragons in Europe

By the 1200s, the description of "dragon" was starting to be used in English, and this is believed to have originated from the Greek word *drakōn*, which was the word traditionally used to describe a large snake. This again reflects the fact that many dragons were portrayed as having a snake-like profile, albeit once again often embellished with the characteristics of other creatures as well. These origins played a part in helping to shape general perceptions of dragons as manifestations of evil. This marks an interesting contrast with the widespread view of dragons in Asia, where they are more commonly considered to be benevolent.

This difference in attitude almost certainly reflects the link with Christianity, as the predominant religion of people in Europe. In the Bible, the snake was regarded as a symbol of temptation and evil, having persuaded Eve to eat the fruit of the tree of knowledge in the Garden of Eden, and she in turn encouraged Adam to do likewise. It is therefore easy to see how this belief in snakes as being evil was then transposed into dragons, which effectively evolved from a serpentine form.

The rise of interest in dragons in Europe at this period in history may not have been entirely coincidental either. It followed the start of the Crusades—a series of military campaigns undertaken by expeditions sent by the Catholic Church, initially to recapture the city of Jerusalem from Muslim rule. This then brought Europeans into closer contact with Asiatic beliefs and thought, and this probably served to reinforce the image of the so-called "draco"—or dragon—in the West.

Indeed, it was at this stage that the typical European view of dragons came into existence, evolving from a variety of sources, which trace back to the original view of dragons as snake-like creatures. This was commonplace during the classical period and extended until Anglo-Saxon times during the eleventh century. Indeed, the famous epic poem of the period, known as *Beowulf*, which was written about 1000 CE by an unknown author, describes a dragon at that stage as resembling a snake-like creature. Indeed, the way it moved was by bending its body, like a snake, as reflected by the use of the Anglo-Saxon verb *bugan*, in addition to displaying other serpent-like similarities.

At the conclusion of the poem, Beowulf, as the hero, is compelled to battle the aggressive dragon, with both of them dying in the ensuing fight. This titanic battle is triggered by the theft of a cup decorated with jewels taken from the dragon's lair.

There are a number of similar sagas, some dating back to an earlier era before Beowulf, featuring the Germanic hero Sigurd (also sometimes referred to as Siegfried) who, according to legend, was responsible for slaying the dragon Fáfnir. It is actually in the Norse sagas therefore, originating from the area of modern-day Scandinavia, that the first known account of a dragon-slayer emerges, in the guise of Sigurd. Stories of this type extend from Nordic countries, through Germany and even to the UK, where there are stone crosses dating to the 1000s commemorating this specific event.

Aside from these secular accounts, dragons also feature in the religious works of the period, called hagiographies, exploring the lives of saints and other significant ecclesiastical figures. Reaching the peak of popularity during the Middle Ages, although dating back as far as early Christian times, these reverential accounts focus on the achievements of such people and were used for congregational teaching purposes by members of the church. Just as in *Beowulf*, there were battles between saints like Saint Elisabeth the Wonderworker of Constantinople and evil dragons, which seemingly became more prominent in such stories from the 800s onward.

In fact, there are also indicators within *Beowulf* not only of how the popular view of the dragon was changing, but also of the increasingly heroic role of the dragon-slayer, who often features in European dragon tales. These accounts provide further confirmation of the more combative relationship that was developing in stories involving people and dragons in Europe at this stage.

The Role of the Dragon Slayer

Although there were a number of other similar accounts involving Christian saints, it is the story of St. George and the dragon that is best known today by far. Yet what is not widely appreciated is that the roots of this story extend back much earlier than the start of the medieval period. Saint Theodore Tiro, also sometimes referred to as Theodore of Amasea, was an early Greek Christian who was burnt to death about 300 CE, having failed to renounce his faith. Images, in the form of iconography on the walls of surviving churches, reveal how the legend of the dragon slayer subsequently evolved. Artwork of this type was very important, as it served to tell stories to the congregation at a time when most people were unable to read or write.

St. Theodore was originally portrayed on horseback and shown holding a military standard bearing the image of a "draco" (which could either be in the form of a dragon or a snake). These particular flags were carried specifically by Roman military units of cavalry known as cohorts.

Down through the subsequent centuries, this imagery evolved and by the tenth century, there is a fresco in the Turkish cave churches at Göreme showing saints battling with a pair of snakes. In the same region of Cappadocia, there is a fresco that portrays St. Theodore alongside St. George fighting against a supposed dragon, again in the guise of a snake, located in the so-called Snake Church or Yılanlı Kilise. This artwork is believed to date back to the same period, although it could even be slightly earlier.

There are other representations of these two saints together in churches elsewhere in Europe, such as close to the village of Kolchida in the central part of Macedonia. Yet, ultimately, it was to be St. George who assumed the role of dragon-slayer, rather than St. Theodore, from the eleventh century onward, for reasons that are unclear. The earliest definitive imagery of St. George in this role that still exists is also to be found in Cappadocia, Turkey, where it is present within the church of Santa Barbara. The dragon in this case once again has a very serpentine form.

There is, however, very little information existing about St. George himself. As George of Lydda, he is believed to have been martyred for his Christian beliefs, having been a member of the Roman army. He probably died about 30 CE, but it was only much later that the legend of St George and the dragon was seemingly told for the first time. The story describes how a dragon was persecuting the residents of the Libyan city of Silene, forcing the local people to offer it two sheep every day, until they had no more sheep left.

The dragon then started to demand people instead, and it reached the point where the king's daughter was due to be sacrificed. Luckily, George arrived at Silene at this stage and took it upon himself to slay the dragon with a long lance while mounted on horseback, before finally beheading it with his sword. The king offered George a reward of treasure for saving his daughter's life, but George declined the offer for himself, insisting that the poor people in the city be helped instead. They in turn expressed their gratitude to George by converting to Christianity.

The story of St. George first featured in a collection of 153 different idealized hagiographies about saints that were originally compiled around 1260 by Jacobus de Voragine, who was the Archbishop of Genoa. It was clearly a very significant work, which ultimately became known as the *Golden Legend*, providing information that could be used by the clergy to explain saints' days to congregations.

Remarkably, over a thousand hand-copied manuscripts still survive, tending to confirm the work's importance, but it was after the development of printing by an Englishman named William Caxton (who is thought to have lived from about 1422 to 1491) that this book assumed even greater significance. Its status at the time was such that it was one of the first books that Caxton printed, and it became one of the earliest titles to be translated as well, ensuring its wide distribution.

The account of St. George and the Dragon featured in this hagiography subsequently captured the imagination of other writers, as well as artists and sculptors. This has helped to ensure that the story has remained alive down through subsequent centuries to the present day. Although St. George is now regarded as the patron saint of England for his dragon slaying, he also features in the mythology and iconography of a wide range of other countries, including on Moscow's coat of arms, as well as those of cities of eighteen other countries across Europe. This legacy has continued, with St. George's dragon killing being incorporated as recently as the last century into the design of the Imperial standard of Emperor Haile Selassie I of Ethiopia (1892–1975).

Representations of St. George are especially common in Spain, where St. George himself is regarded as the patron saint of the Catalonian region. Again, Catalan dragons are portrayed in a variety of forms, but most typically with a serpentine body, four legs, and a pair of wings, albeit with a rather more varied facial shape, likened to a lion in some cases. They were regarded as fire-breathing and also capable of producing a potentially fatal odor that would rot away flesh that it came into contact with, making these dragons particularly dangerous.

Some older portrayals of Catalan dragons feature them as having just two legs. These ultimately evolved into separate types of dragon-like creatures that can be seen on many older buildings in Europe especially. These became known as wyverns, a name derived from the Old French word *wyvre*, which actually translates as "serpent." These became significant symbols in British and French heraldry, being commemorated today, for example, by the appearance of a wyvern on the national flag of Wales.

A long tradition dating right back to ancient Egyptian temples is the portrayal of dragonesque creatures as water spouts on buildings. These came to prominence in the medieval period thanks to a legend that grew up around the French city of Rouen. The local people were effectively under siege from an aggressive dragon called La Gargouille, which would attack boats traveling on the River Seine, as well as flooding the area around the city. Then a priest named Romanus promised the city's inhabitants that if they built a church, he would destroy the dragon. Having done so, St. Romanus, as he would become, attached the dead dragon's head to the city walls. This event was subsequently commemorated by carved stone dragon figures being added to the corners of many important buildings. They are described as gargoyles, commemorating the name of La Gargouille in part, although the range of such creatures portrayed in stone in this way is not confined to representations of dragons, lions also being frequently featured.

Key Differences

Significant distinctions both in the appearance and nature of dragons have subsequently emerged when comparing Asian and European representations. The evolution from a snake-like entity to a more complex creature took place during the Middle Ages in Europe, leading to quite a profound change in the dragon's appearance.

One of the most significant indicators is to be seen in a bestiary—an illustrated natural history of animals—known as *MS Harley 3244*. This manuscript is believed to date from about 1260 and portrays a dragon with a long, narrow body shape, retaining a serpentine appearance as a result but clearly distinguished from those of an earlier era by possessing two pairs of legs and the same number of wings.

It is also seen to be breathing what appears to be fire out of its small mouth, which was the result of its very hot venom. The dragon's tail displays what appears to be a series of thorns along its length. In fact, this was considered to be the most dangerous part of its body, as it could lash out with it and suffocate any creature that it caught.

Dragons, which could be found in both India and Ethiopia, were said to prey especially on elephants by hiding alongside the paths where they walked. This was believed to be why elephants gave birth in water, so as to escape dragons at this stage. In turn, however, dragons themselves could be badly affected by the supposed sweet breath of panthers (leopards) and would seek to hide in caves when they heard the roar of these big cats.

A dragon would also avoid the peridexion tree, being fearful of its shadow. The tree attracted doves to feed on its fruits, but they were safe in its protective shade where they would not be seized by a dragon. As was usual with a bestiary, there was clearly a moral dimension here too. A popular interpretation was that the doves represented Christians, with the tree signifying the nourishment and protection of the church: those who strayed outside would be taken by the devil, represented once more in this case by the dragon. There was symbolism attached to the elephant story too. Dragons ambushed them in the same way that the devil preyed on people, catching the unwary, especially when they were at their most vulnerable.

What is perhaps less well-known today is the belief in dragons as living entities and how parts of their body could be used for therapeutic purposes, rather like a unicorn's horn. Thus, various parts of a dragon's body could be used to combat the fear of ghosts and evil spirits. They had to be boiled in wine, and the potion was then left to cool overnight before being applied to the person's body twice daily.

Dragon's blood was most highly sought after, however, for treating a wide range of ailments including bladder stones. The blood, dissolved in hot water, had to be drunk on an empty stomach, after which the patient needed to eat a meal. Following nine days of such treatment, the stones would reputedly break down, leading to recovery. It was considered to be very important not to drink the dragon's blood undiluted, though, because it was so powerful that it would prove to be deadly.

It was also said that dragons had a translucent stone known as draconites within their brain. This was considered to be very valuable, as a whitish gemstone, but it had to be obtained while the dragon was still alive, otherwise it became soft and dissolved. A hunter would therefore drug a dragon with herbs and cut open its head in order to extract the stone safely.

In the case of the legend of the dragon-slayer Sigurd, the blood of the dragon Fáfnir has an unusual effect, according to Scandinavian legend. Having burnt his finger while he was cooking Fáfnir's heart and sucking it in his mouth to relieve the pain, Sigurd swallows some of the dragon's blood at the same time. It has the unexpected effect of allowing him to understand what the animals are saying. This was probably linked to the belief that the heart was widely believed at that stage to be the part of the body where the soul and memory were located.

It was also thought that if someone bathed in dragon's blood, their skin would become impervious to stab wounds. On the other hand, tempering the blade of a sword with dragon's blood would harden it and might even make it poisonous, like the undiluted blood itself. There was traditionally much more focus on dragon's blood in Western culture, possibly because of its long-standing availability, although in Asia, it was believed that if drops fell on the ground, they would create amber.

The Truth About Dragon's Blood

References to dragon's blood extend back as far as the ancient Romans, being first mentioned in a sailing and trading manual called the *Periplus Maris Erythraei*, translating as "Periplus of the Erythraean Sea," which is believed to date back to around the middle of the first century CE. "Periplus," meaning a sea voyage around a coast, suggests that the area this document covered was basically what we know today as the Indian Ocean. The writer provides a surprisingly accurate account of travel in this area, indicating that it must have been written by someone familiar with the region, although its authorship is unknown.

During the Roman era, dragon's blood was seen as a rare and precious commodity, obtained from the small Yemeni island of Socotra, which lies south of the Arabian Peninsula in the Indian Ocean. It was actually obtained from an endemic tree, which grows nowhere else in the world, known as *Dracaena cinnabari*. This tree yields a red sap when its bark is cut, creating the resin from which dragon's blood is made. It can then be dried and used as a powdered pigment for example.

There was also a particularly dangerous form of dragon's blood known to the Romans, which is described as cinnabar and originates not from plants but is a mineral called mercury sulfide. This is the source of the brilliant red pigment referred to as vermilion in artistic circles. Unfortunately, it is also toxic because of its mercuric component.

Dragon's blood made from plants has been popular with artists for thousands of years. Pliny the Elder, writing in approximately 77 CE, described its value, and it continued to be used to create flesh tones in paintings through the nineteenth century, as well as being a key ingredient in the pigment known as Chinese orange. One of the most famous works incorporating dragon's blood is called the *Pentecost,* by the Italian painter Giotto (c. 1267–1330 CE) which dates back to about 1300. Here it was used to create the appearance of fire above the heads of Jesus's apostles. Dragon's blood subsequently became preferred for use as a varnish rather than as a paint, being used especially on Italian violins—a purpose for which it is still sought-after today.

Perhaps strangely, it was not actually until the medieval period—about one thousand years after it was first described by the Romans—that the belief grew up that this resin actually consisted of the blood of dragons that had died fighting elephants, making it a rare and precious commodity. Later in history, starting in the 1400s, seafarers visiting the Canary Islands on the other side of Africa discovered a new form of the resin, originating from a related plant known as *Dracaena draco.*

This is now the most widely used source today, although other types of dragon's blood have since been found. Rattan palms belonging to the genus *Calamus,* occurring on various Indonesian islands, yield a variant known as "jernang," which in this case is obtained from the protective resin that encases the developing fruit. It is the most commonly available form today, with the resin being rolled for sale into large balls. In China, *Calamus* resin is traditionally favored to add a distinctive red coating on furniture.

In South America, dragon's blood comes from plants belonging to the genus *Croton,* which are widely known there as Sangre de Drago. Again, in this case, it is the sap of the plant that is used. Remarkably, dragon's blood from plants is still used for medicinal purposes today, with studies having confirmed its efficacy at treating various bacterial and fungal infections, as well as aiding the immune system.

Making Sense of Dragons

In spite of the fear that stories surrounding dragons could create, at a time when the natural world was far less well understood than it is today, it is clear that large, dragonesque creatures never existed. They almost certainly evolved from stories about encounters with large serpents, probably pythons, which inhabited both Africa and Asia and were far bigger than snakes found in Europe.

Unfortunately, it is impossible to pinpoint the origins of dragons accurately. Did the myth first arise in Europe or in Asia? Perhaps it arose first in the East and then traveled westward into Europe? Or could the belief have taken root separately on both continents? Similarities do exist, such as the indisputable reptilian element that underpins the appearance of all dragons, but over time, the characteristics of dragons have diverged, with such creatures being seen as much more aggressive in Europe.

Asian dragons in general are viewed as being more benign creatures, which were nevertheless powerful, being able to transform the weather, as part of the natural world. It could be that the fossilized remains of creatures from the era of the dinosaurs contributed to the belief in dragons as living creatures in China especially, which has become recognized as a hotspot for such finds over recent years. People may have identified exposed fossilized remains as being from gigantic living creatures, without realizing their true origins. In order to explain them, a belief in dragons as gigantic, long-lived creatures that dwelt on unreachable mountain peaks and in the sky could have arisen, as a way of explaining why they were not commonly seen. This in turn could have had a lasting influence on the Oriental view of dragons, which has continued through to the present day.

Ten Things You May Not Know About Dragons

1   It is believed that the length of a Chinese dragon will directly affect its power to convey luck. The most extensive yet constructed measured a remarkable 18,390 feet (5,605 m) in overall length, being created during October 2012 in Hong Kong.

2   The dragon Smaug, as portrayed in *Beowulf*, inspired J. R. R. Tolkien's work *The Hobbit*, which was published during 1937—nearly a thousand years later.

3   The operatic composer Richard Wagner took the legend of Sigurd the dragon slayer as part of his inspiration for the opera *Der Ring des Nibelungen*. It forms the third part of his four-part work known in English as *The Ring Cycle*.

4   The lance with which St. George slew the dragon was given the name of Ascalon, commemorating the ancient city of Ashkelon, which today lies in Israel.

5   The Azhdarchidae family name given to a group of pterosaurs—extinct flying reptiles that lived at the time of the dinosaurs—stems from the Persian word for "dragon," which is *azhdar*. These giants could have a wingspan of up to 39 feet (12 m).

6   Dragon-boat racing has become a very popular sport over recent years. Even the Prince and Princess of Wales took part in a race of this type on a trip in 2023 to Canada.

7   Dragon fruit, which originates from the *Selenicereus* cactus, is so-called because of its skin, which has a leather-like texture with scaly spikes and has been likened to that of a dragon.

8   Asiatic gliding lizards have been given the scientific name of *Draco*—reflecting their miniature dragonesque appearance, although they only grow to less than 8 inches (20 cm) overall. In mythology, smaller dragons are described as dragonets.

9   More than two hundred dragonesque brooches, which served as functional fasteners, have been unearthed from sites in Roman Britain. These date to between 75 and 175 CE and acquired their name because some believe they may bear a resemblance to dragons.

10 In China, the emperor was regarded as being a descendant of a dragon, while in the case of the Chinese Zodiac, the Year of the Dragon is the fifth year of the twelve-year cycle and is considered to be a particularly auspicious year for pregnancies.

4

THE RISE OF THE PHOENIX

Phoenix wall carving at a temple.
Photo courtesy carekung/www.shutterstock.com

While its origins date back thousands of years, the phoenix still serves as a very powerful symbol of rebirth even today. Typically portrayed in the form of a bird, the phoenix is closely associated with fire. Its name probably originates from languages spoken in the Arabic region and appears to be linked to the bright red color of a dye derived from the roots of a plant called common madder (*Rubia tinctorum*).

Early Records

The phoenix was first described by the Greek writer Hesiod in the eighth century BCE. He referred to it as the Arabian or Egyptian bird, which was believed to be its area of distribution. The roots of the phoenix story may extend back even further, however, to the Bennu, a bird that featured in the ancient Egyptian *Book of the Dead*, dating back as far as 1600 BCE. Its appearance at that stage was more like that of a long-legged wading bird, such as an ibis or heron, both of which can be found in this part of the world. In subsequent accounts, however, the phoenix assumes an eagle-like form.

Reports of the phoenix are included in the *Periegesis*, which was written around the turn of the sixth century BCE by Hecataeus of Miletus, and then in *The Histories* by Herodotus, which first appeared in 440 BCE. He describes it as being a great rarity, only seen when the old phoenix dies, which was reportedly just once every five hundred years. Herodotus makes no claim for seeing the phoenix himself, though, and actually questions how the bird could fly from Arabia carrying its ancestor, covered in myrrh, to be interred at the Altar of the Sun.

Appearance and Lifestyle

These early descriptions nevertheless provide details about its appearance, the phoenix being most commonly portrayed as having a scarlet body with iridescent wings, sea-blue eyes, and purplish legs and feet. It had a distinctive tuft of plumage at the back of the head. Other accounts suggest it was a long-tailed bird, distinguishable by its golden head contrasting with its plum-colored body and scarlet back and wings. A large bird, it approximated to the size and appearance of an eagle. A less commonly accepted view of the phoenix was of a bird that was a rich purple in color, with a contrasting golden head and neck. It was believed to possess an attractive song and was naturally quite tame.

One of the most significant accounts of the phoenix is given by the Roman writer Pliny the Elder (c. 23–79 CE). He even described a supposed bird of this type that was brought from Egypt in 47 CE and placed on public display at the Comitium of the Roman Forum, which was a public meeting center, to mark the eight-hundredth anniversary of the founding of the city of Rome. Pliny drew heavily on the experiences of a Roman senator named Manilius, who described the amazing beauty of the phoenix in terms of its coloration. He observed that this was hard to describe, but noted that those from Arabia surpassed their relatives from Ethiopia and India in terms of beauty, indicating that two or possibly three forms were recognized.

Pliny also recorded Manilius's observations that at the end of its long life, the phoenix would create a nest, built from the twigs of aromatic trees, notably those of cinnamon and frankincense and would add numerous sweet-smelling spices within. The actual lifespan of the phoenix has been open to debate according to the early classical writers. Pliny himself recorded its lifespan as being 660 years, while Tacitus stated it could be either 500 years, or alternatively 1,461 years, based on the Egyptian Sothic calendar, and he recorded two previous sightings. A later writer, the Roman historian Cassius Dio (c. 165–235 CE), documented an appearance of the phoenix that had taken place in 36 CE, drawing on the information supplied to Pliny the Elder.

After its death, the new phoenix would arise from the bones of its ancestor, changing from a small worm-creature to gain its spectacular appearance. Pliny then reiterated the story of the phoenix flying with the remains of its ancestor to place it on the Altar of the Sun. However, he dismissed the report of the phoenix being brought to Rome and seen by a hall full of people, suggesting that this bird was an interloper, rather than the real phoenix.

The Beginning of the End in Reality

It appears that belief in the phoenix declined from this point onward in Rome. Tacitus (56–120 CE) was one of the writers who highlighted the exaggeration and doubt that surrounded reports of the phoenix, although he still stated categorically that it could be seen occasionally in Egypt. He claimed its last appearance had been in 34 CE, but nevertheless, his writing indicates there is a distinct change in attitude toward belief in the phoenix, at this relatively early stage in history.

The only supposed physical evidence of the phoenix came from the Musaeum Tradescantianum, which was the first museum opened to the public in England. Created by John Tradescant the Elder (c. 1570–1638) along with his son, this collection of curiosities was located in a building called The Ark, in the area of South Lambeth, London. Among the oddities on view here were a pair of feathers that had supposedly originated from a phoenix, although how and when they were acquired is unknown. When his son, also called John, passed away in 1662, the collection passed to Elias Ashmole and ultimately became part of the Ashmolean Museum in Oxford, although it appears that these feathers disappeared from the collection at some stage during the intervening years.

The first attempt to classify all animals and plants on the planet was undertaken by the Swedish biologist Carl Linnaeus (1707–1778), who was also known as Carl von Linné. He introduced the binomial ("two name") form of scientific nomenclature for species that is still followed today. Linnaeus included the phoenix within the second edition of his monumental work called the *Systema Naturae*, which was published in 1740.

However, it featured not in the main listing but under the Animalia Paradoxa heading, along with other contentious creatures. These included the siren as well as draco (or dragon), which Linnaeus described as having the body of a snake, combined with feet and the wings of a bat, although in reality, he proposed that this could have been a distorted ray or lizard. Linnaeus was apparently equally unconvinced by the existence of the phoenix as an avian species. He believed there had been major confusion over its identity, which stemmed from an ancient Mycenean Greek word, and it was in reality the date palm, still classified today under its generic name of *Phoenix*!

Although it had achieved official recognition of a sort, this then essentially marked the end of any belief in the phoenix as a living bird. Nevertheless, the story of the phoenix has captured human imagination, to the extent that it has remained a potent image in the public consciousness to the present day. This is reflected in English phrases such as "rising like a phoenix," effectively meaning being reborn, as in the case of an idea or plan.

Possible Identities

On this basis, it would clearly be easy to dismiss the phoenix as nothing more than a mythological bird, dreamed up in classical times. Yet as we have seen already, in the case of the unicorn, for example, accounts of mysterious creatures often have their roots in reality. What clear advantage would belief in the phoenix bring? It seems evident that even if its life was not fully understood, there was a view that this bird actually existed. It raises the question as to whether descriptions of the phoenix could be based in part on a living bird.

In fact, there is actually a very convincing candidate that corresponds closely to written descriptions of the phoenix in various respects. Its origins lie much farther to the east, beyond the accepted boundaries of the classical world, in the mountainous forests of western China. Its coloration matches that of the described appearance of the phoenix to a significant extent, and it is in fact one of the most spectacularly colored birds in the world. When you see it fly, with its long tail streaming out behind its body, it not only looks truly spectacular, but it is also much bigger than might otherwise be suspected.

The golden pheasant (*Chrysolophus pictus*) apparently remained unknown to science for centuries after initial reports of the phoenix, however, being first classified again by the taxonomist Carl Linnaeus, in the tenth edition of his famous book *Systema Naturae*, published in 1758. This was eighteen years after he had recognized and dismissed the existence of the phoenix in an earlier edition. It is only the male bird that displays such striking coloration, however, with females having brownish plumage barred with black. With their long tails, they can measure up to 41 inches (105 cm) in overall length.

There is another highly significant reason to believe that this pheasant may correspond to the phoenix of ancient times. The adaptable nature of such birds, which can be fed on grain, means that individuals could quite easily have been traded and transported alive to Rome, for example, where they would have been viewed with wonder.

This seems the most likely explanation of Pliny's report of a phoenix being displayed to visitors to the Comitium of the Roman Forum in 47 CE. On this basis, the phoenix can be explained simply as a case of mistaken identity. Such would be the incredible scarcity of sightings of such birds in Europe at that

Golden pheasant in flight.
Photo courtesy Wang LiQiang/www.shutterstock.com

time in history that it is easy to see how a legend could have evolved about their life history and lifespan as well.

An alternative but far less convincing suggestion is that confusion with flamingos could lie behind the phoenix's identity. It is true that the two Old World species of flamingo are a pinkish-red in coloration, mimicking its fiery shade to an extent, but other than that, there is little in common between the appearance of these long-legged flamingos and that of the phoenix.

The greater flamingo (*Phoenicopterus roseus*) has a wide range across much of southern Europe into Asia, while its smaller cousin, known as the lesser flamingo (*Phoeniconaias minor*) occurs in parts of Africa, such as the Great Rift Valley and can also be found in an area of northwestern India. The distribution of both species therefore actually indicates that it is unlikely that these birds were confused with tales of the phoenix. They would clearly have been known in many parts of the ancient world, including Egypt, Greece, and Italy, whereas the phoenix, first and foremost, was a bird of wonder and mystery, being a great rarity and quite unlike anything that people in Europe had seen before.

A further point that undermines the suggestion that a flamingo could explain the phoenix's identity is the highly specialized diet of these birds, which feed on tiny crustaceans that they filter out of the water. This means that they could not have been kept alive easily, either during transport or indeed, while on display in Rome, as was seemingly the case, based on Pliny's account. A pheasant feeding on grain, however, would have been much easier to maintain successfully.

Other Similar Accounts

There are other accounts of phoenix-like birds from various parts of Asia. They include the Persian simurgh, which, according to Iranian legend, can live for up to 1,700 years before it dies in flames and is then reborn. It reputedly possessed all the knowledge passed down through the ages because it lived so long. There are various depictions of the simurgh, which was said to be partly mammalian because it suckled its young. Other portrayals consider it to be a large eagle-like bird known to have a dislike of snakes.

Closely associated with water, the simurgh would fly to the middle of the world's sea where it roosted on the gaokerena. This tree was considered to possess healing powers, bestowing eternal life on those who drank the juice of its fruit. The simurgh was seemingly less connected to the sun than the phoenix and rather more to the celestial cosmos in general, acting as a link to the earth. Just as with the phoenix today, however, the simurgh remains a potent symbol in Iranian culture, appearing in media ranging from books and films to video games.

Another mythical bird of Iranian origins distinct from the simurgh is variously known as the homa, homay, or huma. Once again, it is often portrayed as having a pheasant-like appearance, including long, trailing tail plumes. Sightings were believed to be auspicious, but this was a bird that never landed and spent its entire existence above the clouds. Huma are often portrayed without legs for this reason. In common with other phoenix-like birds, it reputedly lived for hundreds of years and possessed the ability to regenerate itself after having been consumed by fire. Another legend is that it could convey kingship. This belief extended from beyond ancient Persia, being retold in stories from the Indian Mughal Empire, which came into existence in the 1500s and lasted until 1857.

Birds of Paradise

Interestingly, the huma is often described as a bird of paradise in Ottoman poetry, a name given to birds with stunning plumage that originate from New Guinea and surrounding islands. Initially, they were believed not to perch either, simply because the skins that the early explorers obtained and sent back to scientific institutions had no legs attached.

Birds of paradise (forming the family Paradisaeidae) were first encountered on New Guinea by the crew of Ferdinand Magellan's expedition during their circumnavigation of the globe, which had set sail from Spain in 1519. It was initially believed that they may have discovered the land of the phoenix in New Guinea, given the stunning beauty of these birds, combined with their supposed lack of legs, which suggested they remained consistently airborne throughout their lives.

Roots in China?

Within Asia itself, there are also various accounts of mythological bird-like entities that bear a resemblance to the phoenix, although these are less well-known in the West. China, for example, is reputedly the home of the Fenghuang, sometimes recorded as Fung-Whang. The name originally represented a combination of a male bird (reflected by Feng) and a female (Huang). Yet, over time, Fenghuang (which is pronounced *fung-khwaang*) became increasingly viewed as a female entity, being closely associated with the Chinese dragon, which is regarded as being male.

The bird represents fire, and portrayals clearly resemble a golden pheasant in appearance. Indeed, its traditional colors of red, yellow, azure, white, and black correspond closely to that of this pheasant. Closely linked with the unicorn in Chinese mythology, sightings of this creature were said to be rare—another link to the story of the phoenix in Western culture. It was only likely to be seen in areas of peace and prosperity. In addition, it was accorded a close link to fire, often being portrayed with fire surrounding it. The home of the Fenghuang was reportedly in the Kunlun Mountains, which lie in the western part of China.

The earliest known example of the Fenghuang dates back to eight thousand years ago, with a design of this type being unearthed in Hunan Province. Could it be that the story of the phoenix arose in China and then reached Europe, or as with dragons, could there be two separate origins in this case?

The Japanese Influence

In Japan, there is a mythological bird-like creature called the hōō, better known in the West as the HoHo bird. Its images decorate the imperial throne, commemorating its appearance there, when its attractive song was credited with bringing harmony and prosperity to the country. It is viewed as a symbol of rebirth and as a messenger of the sun goddess known as Amaterasu.

Once again, the hōō is brightly colored, just like the phoenix, with red, gold, and green plumage, as well as black and white areas, which are linked to the five fundamental colors. It has a crest of longer feathers on its head and flowing tail plumes, which, again, calls to mind the image of a pheasant overall. Although there is a type of pheasant called the green pheasant (*Phasianus versicolor*) that is present in Japan, it is far less colorful that its Chinese cousin, and it seems likely that the roots of the hōō may therefore lie in China.

Often portrayed among cherry trees, the hōō feeds on the seeds of bamboo—which only appear every seven years. Its favorite nesting site is said to be within the branches of paulownia trees, commonly described as *kiri* in its homeland.

The influence of the hōō spread much more widely outside Japan, however, leaving a lasting legacy in the design of furniture and other decorative objects. In the 1800s in Europe, the hoho bird became a common feature on mirrors and other furniture during the Rococo and subsequent Georgian periods, particularly items designed in a Japanese style, with lacquered wood.

Heading South into Korea

There are also a number of phoenix-like figures represented in Korean mythology, with the best known being the bonghwang (봉황). It is possible to distinguish different animals in its appearance, but again, much of its body is predominantly bird-like, although in this case, its tail is more like that of a fish. Again, though, it is said to be surrounded by bright light and reflects the balance between yin and yang, as well as often being linked to dragons. Different areas of its body are linked with celestial phenomena; its wings evoke the wind, for example, while its eyes mirror the sun. The bonghwang is more closely associated with cosmic harmony overall, rather than the death and rebirth cycle that typifies the phoenix in the West.

The bonghwang also displays a strong link with royalty, being closely linked particularly to the female line, and it is seen as a symbol around palaces and featured in the design of royal garments. Today, its image is included in the presidential seal of South Korea, where it serves to indicate the resilient spirit of the country's people. It remains a potent symbol in the country's culture. A station named after the bonghwang even features on the Busan Metro line.

Other less-known phoenix-like entities feature in Korean mythology as well. They include the so-called vermilion bird (or jujak), which represents fire and so could be more closely aligned with the phoenix itself. It is always portrayed as a fiery red bird.

The other member of this group is the so-called inmyeonjo (인면조), which is distinguishable in part by its typically female, human-like face, combined with the body of a bird, symbolizing the connection between the earth and sky. Portrayals of the inmyeonjo dating back some 1,500 years have been found in Buddhist tombs of the Three Kingdoms period. Furthermore, a modern-day representation was featured at the opening ceremony of the Winter Olympics held in 2018 in Pyeongchang, South Korea, reflecting its enduring cultural significance.

Ten Things You May Not Know About the Phoenix

1 The city of Phoenix, Arizona, owes its name to the legendary bird. The modern city is built on land formerly occupied for about two thousand years by the Hohokam people. They had been forced to abandon the area about 1400 CE because of drought, leaving their irrigation canals empty.

2   The name *Phoenix* was proposed by one of the city's first settlers, an Englishman born in Paris who styled himself as Lord Darrell Duppa (1832–1892) and who helped to pioneer the city's development from 1867 onward.

3   In Slavic mythology, the mythical firebird has parallels to the phoenix, but in this case, it takes the form of a falcon, being recognized as a symbol of masculinity. The firebird's existence is closely linked to the seasons, with its rebirth occurring each spring.

4   In China, the phoenix's links with beauty and felinity resulted in it being portrayed as a symbol of the Chinese empress.

5   During the early days of Christianity, the phoenix was regarded as a symbol of the death and resurrection of Christ, and as a result, it was frequently featured on tombstones at that stage in history.

6   There is a group of stars in the southern hemisphere, first identified in 1603, that take the form of a bird and these have been named the Phoenix constellation.

7   The famous opera house in the Italian city of Venice is La Fenice, and it has strangely lived up to its name, which translates as The Phoenix. This is because it has burnt down twice in its history—in 1836 and subsequently in 1996—and has been rebuilt on both occasions.

8   Jewish mythology features a phoenix-like entity called the milcham bird. Its origins trace back to the Garden of Eden, where Eve, having persuaded Adam to eat the forbidden fruit, then offered some to other creatures living there, being jealous of their immortality. The milcham bird, also referred to as the hoi in the Bible, declined, and it was rewarded by God with a home in a safe walled city, where it could live for one thousand years before being reborn.

9   There are numerous symbols of historical references in place names relating to the phoenix. Atlanta, the capital city of the US state of Georgia, features a phoenix on its flag and city seal, reflecting how it was rebuilt from ashes after being torched by General Sherman's army during the American Civil War.

10 The phoenix features in many songs. One of the most successful was the title track of the 1979 double platinum-selling album simply titled *Phoenix*, by US singer-songwriter Dan Fogelberg. The cover artwork also featured a phoenix in this case.

5

VANQUISHING VAMPIRES

A cross and garlic, which are both widely believed to repel vampires.
Photo courtesy Roselynne/www.shutterstock.com

Nocturnal, blood-sucking entities have inspired fear among people for millennia, dating back to ancient times, with accounts to be found in almost every culture worldwide. One of the earliest known representations of such beings feeding on the blood of people has been unearthed on shards of Persian pottery believed to have been made around 400 BCE.

These creatures take different forms, but they were universally viewed as evil spirits that were most likely to be active under cover of darkness. People in ancient Babylonia—the area that encompasses modern day Iraq, as well as parts of Iran and Syria—told of Lilitu, a demon who sought to drink the blood of young babies. Hebrew folklore featured a very similar nocturnal entity, known as Lilith, the name translating as "night monster."

Early Manifestations

Representations of Lilith have been found on amulets and incantation bowls dating from the first to the eighth centuries CE, confirming that she was a potent demonic figure. In addition, there were the much-feared estries, who fed on blood, and were similar to the succubae, which were female demons. Both groups could manifest as people, and yet they were also able to shape shift, particularly in the case of estries, which often appeared in the guise of animals such as cats. The name *estrie* derives from the Latin *strix*, meaning owl—a bird that comes to life after dark.

Should an estrie become injured, she could recover if able to drink blood, or if assisted, by being given bread and salt. Reflecting a link extending to modern vampires, it was widely recognized that after death, an estrie could not simply be buried. Otherwise, she would come back to life. The estrie's corpse needed to have its mouth filled with soil, or it could alternatively be decapitated or burnt.

The succubae were reputed to feed primarily on the blood of women and babies, although they were also thought to attack men on occasions. Over the course of history, however, it appears that the actions of the succubae changed, eventually becoming viewed as sirens rather than vampires.

The Rise of the Vampire

The origins of modern vampiric beliefs can be traced back to the southeastern part of Europe in the 1700s. The use of the word *vampyre* was first recorded in English in 1732, subsequently morphing into the current spelling of "vampire," although its exact origins are unclear. It is thought to be derived from Slavic or Turkic languages.

There was a massive upsurge in concern about vampires at this stage in history, starting in what is now modern-day Serbia. It was triggered initially by the passing of a peasant named Petar Blagojević, who died in 1725 at the age of sixty-two. In the small village where he lived, there followed a spate of other deaths. Nine people died unexpectedly and suddenly within the course of the next eight days. Remarkably, as they lay dying, each person stated that Blagojević had come to strangle them in the night.

Other stories involved Blagojević's immediate family. His wife apparently claimed that after his death, he returned to ask for his shoes, causing her to move from their home. Another report suggested that he had come back and asked his son for food. In a fit of anger when refused, Blagojević had then supposedly killed him and drank his blood.

The growing fear in the area created widespread unrest, and with local people demanding answers, the authorities realized that they had to act. An official named Ernst Frombald became involved, ultimately writing a report about what had happened. In a very early case of press coverage, the Austrian newspaper known as *Wiennerisches Diarium* (which still publishes today as *Wiener Zeitung*) picked up the story.

Unfortunately, the situation became even worse the following year, as a result of the death of a man named Arnold Paole, who had claimed to have suffered as the victim of a vampire. Nevertheless, he reportedly said that he had cured himself by visiting its grave, digging up the corpse and covering his body with its blood, as well as swallowing soil from the grave.

When Paole himself died in a fall from a hay wagon, people were immediately concerned. Their fears grew as four other people died within a month; all of them were on record as stating that Paole had made them ill. The belief soon spread rapidly that he himself had been a vampire.

A government official who had previous experience of vampires was consulted. Paole's grave was opened, and in his coffin, to the horror of those present, they observed that his body had not decomposed, although he had been dead for forty days. Worse still, there was fresh blood flowing out of his eyes, as well as his mouth, ears, and nose. The interior of the coffin had become stained with blood, while his nails, as well as his beard and hair, had apparently grown since his death.

These were all signs known to be associated with vampires. The villagers acted accordingly, plunging a stake through his heart and causing an apparent chilling shriek to be emitted by the corpse. They then decapitated Paole's body and burnt his remains, doing the same with his supposed victims, hoping to prevent them from becoming vampires.

Further Cases

in the winter of 1730–1731, there was then another alarming outbreak of vampirism reported in the same area. Two Austrian doctors named Flückinger and Glaser, who were sent to investigate, wrote a detailed report. The source of the outbreak in this case was believed to be an older woman named Milica. Within a few weeks, ten people of various ages were dead, with the casualties including a young woman named Stana, who had died in childbirth. Both she and Milica had moved to the village from elsewhere. Milica had admitted eating mutton from sheep killed by Paole and the other vampires five years beforehand, while Stana had previously said that she had covered herself in vampire blood as protection, because they were widespread in the area where she used to live.

Once again, the case caused widespread panic among local people, bordering on mass hysteria according to some accounts. This led to Glaser, as a specialist in infectious diseases, carrying out an assessment of the situation. He arranged for the bodies of the deceased to be disinterred and was shocked to discover that a dozen of them, including those of people who had died first, showed no signs of decomposition. Even worse, they had liquid blood in their mouths.

Glaser recommended that in accordance with the wishes of the local people, the vampires should be destroyed. The authorities responded by organizing a further investigation, resulting in three military surgeons and two army officers visiting the graves almost a month later, in January 1731. These were opened, and the findings were very similar to those of the previous investigation, in spite of more time having passed.

Their report noted the growth of new fingernails, and the vivid red appearance of the skin. There could only be one conclusion: these corpses were clearly affected by vampirism. They were therefore decapitated and burnt, with the ashes being thrown into a local river in the hope of preventing any further cases arising, while the other unaffected bodies were laid to rest.

The fact that the official findings into the incident accepted the explanation of vampirism meant that there was now formal recognition that vampires existed. Rather than calming the situation, therefore, as the authorities hoped, this simply led to greater concern.

A number of texts were written at this stage investigating vampirism, including the influential *Treatise on the Apparitions of Spirits and on Vampires or Revenants of Hungary, Moravia and Silesia*, which was originally published in two volumes in 1746 by Antoine Augustin Calmet (1672–1757) who was an academic and a French Benedictine monk. A second edition, endorsed by the king of France, then appeared five years later, emphasizing the importance placed on this topic.

In his coverage of vampires, Calmet distinguished between them and phantoms or ghosts, which had no physical presence. In spite of taking a critical, analytical approach to the subject, he evidently struggled to refute the concept of vampirism. He listed many cases of vampirism that were well known at the time, including a case from 1730, reported by a soldier who was staying at the home of a peasant. They were talking over the dinner and were joined in the middle of the meal by another man, who sat down quietly and did not introduce himself, although his presence seemed to disturb the soldier's host. The next morning, the soldier found his host unexpectedly dead.

Having reported this information to his regimental commanders, a team which included a senior officer and a surgeon were tasked with carrying out an investigation. Local residents believed that the mysterious visitor was in fact the man's long-dead father, and it was decided to disinter his body. Horrifyingly, there was no apparent sign of decomposition of the corpse, in spite of the fact that it had been buried for a decade, and worse still, it apparently had the blood flow of a living person.

There was reportedly a very similar case involving a man who had died thirty years before and then apparently returned while family members were eating. The vampire drew blood from the neck of his brother on the first occasion, then from a son, and finally on his third visitation from a servant, all of whom died instantly. The exhumation revealed the same findings as in the previous case, but rather than decapitate the corpse in this instance, as happened previously, a nail was driven through the temple of the man's head, after which it was placed back in its grave.

Looking at the Evidence Today

Faced with such overwhelming testimony from seemingly reliable witnesses, including surgeons and senior military figures, it was difficult for Calmet to rebut these assertions at that stage. But could there actually be other explanations? Back then, the processes underlying decomposition of bodies were not understood. A number of factors influence the speed of a body's breakdown, such as temperature for example, not to mention the soil type. A body buried in winter in freezing ground is unlikely to decay as fast as if it were interred in the summer.

Gases in the body can transform its appearance too, causing swelling, so that a body looks fatter than was the case in life, suggesting the corpse may have put on weight. This was noted in the case of one of the women involved in the Arnold Paole case. Associated pressure changes result in blood trickling out of the nose and elsewhere. In fact, as we now know, all these described characteristics associated with vampirism can be accounted for by *post-mortem* changes.

Even the appearance of "growing" fingernails fits into this category, as the skin around the fingers retracts, making them appear as if they are longer than in life. Then finally, if the body is punctured with a stake—which became a traditional method for dealing with vampires—the accumulated gases within will escape and may cause a sound resembling moaning, making it appear as if the vampire has just died.

There was also a difficulty at that period in history in terms of determining accurately when someone had died. Almost certainly, a few individuals suffered the gruesome fate of being buried alive, before reviving once they had been interred. This would account for fingernail marks on the underside of a coffin lid, as the unfortunate person desperately attempted to draw attention to his or her plight and claw their way out. Ultimately, they would have ended up being suffocated while entombed underground.

Another cause of cases of vampirism at that stage in history was the lack of knowledge and understanding surrounding infectious diseases and their spread. Their impact would also have been generally more severe in Europe back then, giving the malnourished state of much of the population. Interestingly, when Glaser was investigating the Serbian vampire incidents, he actually suggested that malnutrition in the population could be a factor, exacerbated by the fasting that formed part of the Eastern Orthodox Christian religion.

Notable winter killers that we recognize today, such as the influenza virus, could easily account for sudden clusters of unexplained deaths in localized communities, affecting people of all ages. Respiratory infections can also cause the regurgitation of blood after death, and close contact with an infected person would obviously have put family members, friends, and close associates at risk. It has also been suggested that cholera outbreaks may have been responsible for outbreaks of deaths in communities, at a time when sanitation was poor.

Contemporary Beliefs Surrounding Vampires

There was widespread concern that after someone died their spirit could be taken over and possessed by another entity. Bodies therefore had to be protected prior to burial, and if there were any obvious signs of injury, these areas had to be purified by pouring boiling water over them. Perhaps strangely, both dogs and cats in particular had to be kept away from corpses. The belief grew up that if they could jump over a corpse, it would then be resurrected as a vampire on the following night. Such thinking might possibly have arisen from the fact that both these animals could have been tempted to feed on the remains, as back then, they were often forced to scavenge, at least in part, for their food.

A number of other beliefs became established too, as people actively sought to protect themselves from the perceived dangers that vampires posed. It was widely believed that vampires could not enter a dwelling without being invited inside. As a precautionary measure therefore, residents would resort to placing a mirror of some sort near the door so that they could see who was wanting to come into their home. This was because it was commonly thought that vampires were unable to cast a shadow, and so they could be distinguished in this way from regular visitors and excluded as a result.

There was also a rather unusual belief that vampires were obsessed with counting. As a result, additional protection could be achieved by leaving large sacks full of seeds of some sort by the door. Mustard was considered especially valuable for this purpose, and it might also be sprinkled over the roof of the dwelling as well. The vampire would be distracted by the counting process, and as a result would fail to retreat before sunrise; this could then be fatal for them.

It was frequently believed that vampires could only live in the dark and were killed by exposure to sunlight. Especially when it was thought that there was an outbreak of vampiric activity in an area, the local authorities would therefore often impose a curfew, with the aim of keeping their citizens safe.

If people found themselves out at night, however, they needed to seek the protection of hallowed ground such as a church, where vampires dared not go. If someone was worried that a vampire was following them, then they were advised to wade through flowing water such as a stream, which the vampire would not be able to cross.

Additional protection for a person could be achieved by carrying what were known as apotropaic items. Since vampires were evil, so the thinking was that they would be driven away by religious artifacts: today, a crucifix is popularly believed to be the strongest deterrent for vampires, but others that were used back then included Holy Water, rosaries, and even images of Jesus Christ. In terms of plants, garlic (*Allium ursinum*) has captured the imagination as the best way to ward off vampires, but hedgerow plants, in the form of hawthorn (*Crataegus monogyna*) and wild rose (*Rosa* species), were also believed to provide valuable protection.

Slaying Vampires

A range of different ways of actually destroying vampires, as distinct from simply deterring them, were devised, with a stake being driven through the heart considered to be a highly effective method. As mentioned previously, this actually allows the escape of gases arising from decomposition within the body, causing it to deflate, with the accompanying sound being likened to a deathly groan.

Aspen (*Populus tremula*), a type of poplar wood, was widely favored for such stakes, as it was believed to have been the wood chosen to construct the cross on which Christ was crucified, giving it extra religious significance and power. Other woods could be used nevertheless, with ash (*Fraxinus*), for example, being more widely employed for this purpose in the Baltic States and Russia.

Sharp farm implements such as sickles were placed next to the body in some burials, in the belief that if a vampire began to develop in the tomb, then this would pierce the skin as its body expanded, destroying the creature. Decapitation was carried out as well, with the head being buried separately in the grave from the body. This was thought to encourage the departure of the soul, which would otherwise remain for longer in the corpse.

Other grave rituals were used to protect bodies from the risk of becoming vampires, in what were known as "anti-vampire burials." These extend back as far as the early medieval period and are generally focused on physically preventing the body from rising up out of the grave. Measures that were taken include stabbing the corpse through the heart with sharp needles made of iron or steel and also pinning it down more generally with pieces of metal to be sure that it could not move.

Plants again played a part in such practices, with hawthorn, for example, being used by the Roma (Romani) people in middle Europe. Sharpened branches were employed to pin the legs down, or lengths were simply added next to the body. Garlic too was used, being placed in the mouth of the deceased in what is now Romania, whereas lemon was the preferred choice in parts of Germany when vampirism was suspected. It was also believed to be possible to kill vampires by shooting, and up until the 1800s, firing a bullet through the coffin of the deceased was standard practice to ensure that the corpse did not morph into a vampire.

In cases where vampirism was suspected, burning the body was considered to be effective in terms of preventing the vampire from running amok. A particularly unpleasant variation, however, involved mixing the ashes of the deceased with water, creating a drink that was then given to other family members to consume as a way of protecting themselves.

Restoring Public Confidence

The authorities soon realized that they had to get a grip on the various vampire stories that were circulating, seemingly after these had gained official approval in the first part of the 1700s. Empress Maria Theresa (1717–1780) dispatched her own trusted personal physician, who was a Dutchman named Gerard van Swieten (1700–1772), to overcome the superstition that by then had become widespread. In his report, which was published in 1768, he lambasted accounts of vampires and explained alleged reports of vampiric involvement in deaths with scientific facts, setting out why, for example, bodies change in appearance after being buried. His findings led directly to new laws banning the exhumation and defilement of bodies because of vampiric fears.

Although widespread concern about vampires had largely died out by the late 1800s in Europe, they remained potent mythological figures. Indeed, there was a case of mass hysteria surrounding vampirism in the town of Exeter, Rhode Island, at this stage, forming part of what has become known as the New England Vampire Panic.

The bacterial disease known as tuberculosis was still a major killer at that stage, often being better known as consumption. It was spread by living in unsanitary conditions, and there was then no treatment available, in the pre-antibiotic era. The infection resulted in a slow and highly unpleasant death, with the victim wasting away and, significantly, in the latter stages of the disease often coughing up blood. Its cause was unknown at that stage, but the illness spread easily among family members living in homes together, as they were in close proximity to each other. The belief grew that a victim who was suffering from this malady was responsible for draining the lives of other family members, who subsequently fell ill.

This was the thinking behind what became known as the Mercy Brown vampire incident, which involved the family members of George and Mary

Brown who were beset by tuberculosis. George's wife, Mary, died first, followed by Mary Olive, who was their eldest daughter, and then her sister Mercy.

With their son Edwin also infected at this stage, speculation in the local community was rife that one of the family had to be a vampire. Although he did not believe in vampirism, George Brown reluctantly agreed to exhumations of their bodies, as a means of quelling local speculation. Unfortunately, this did nothing of the sort, because two months after she had died in January 1892, the body of Mercy was found to be almost totally intact, and an autopsy revealed liquid blood was still present in her heart.

In a gruesome ritual, her heart and liver were therefore removed and burnt, and Edwin was provided with a curative potion comprised of the ashes of his sister's organs mixed with water. It was to no avail: he died just two months afterwards. The truth of the case is that with Mercy dying during the winter, her body being stored in a freezing crypt, there was little opportunity for decomposition to take effect in the period up until her exhumation.

Ironically, and in what must have been a very painful experience, George Brown himself not only escaped the ravage of tuberculosis, but also lived to see the introduction of the BCG vaccine which helps to protect against this disease in 1921. Brown died the following year, but just six years later, Alexander Fleming (1881–1955) discovered penicillin, opening the path for actual medical treatment of cases of tuberculosis.

Continuing Fascination, If Not Fear

Any talk of vampires had by then finally been vanquished by medical science. But the image of vampires lives on, in popular culture. Many writers have been subsequently drawn to the topic of vampires, perhaps most notably John William Polidori (1795–1821), who was Lord Byron's physician and thus became a member of what became known as the Romantic Movement. The pair traveled on what was to be a momentous journey to Switzerland, where they shared a villa on the shore of Lake Geneva with the poet Percy Bysshe Shelley (1792–1822) and his future wife, the writer Mary Wollstonecraft Godwin (1797–1851). Shelley and Godwin had eloped together, with her stepsister, Jane ("Claire") Clairmont, who inspired the trip and was actually pregnant with Byron's child at that stage.

Trapped indoors there for several days in June of 1816, in the notorious year without a summer, when much of Europe and North America was being constantly drenched in rain, the group decided to stay indoors. Each member of the group took turns reading from the French anthology of ghost stories titled *Fantasmagoriana*, which had been translated from the German.

Following on from that, Byron (1788–1824) then suggested that they should each write a ghost story. He himself started his contribution featuring a character named Augustus Darvell. It was written in the form of a letter, documenting an account of traveling with Darvell as an old man who is clearly sick. When they reach a cemetery in Turkey, Darvell passes away, but significantly, only once he has reached an agreement with the narrator of the story not to reveal his death. The man is shocked to see how quickly the body of his traveling companion decomposes, with his face becoming blackish in minutes. He buries the body in the cemetery.

Known as *The Fragment*, that is as far as Byron got in telling the story, before seemingly losing interest in completing it. Polidori, however, was inspired to develop another version of the tale, in the knowledge that Byron intended to show that Darvell was in fact a vampire. In Polidori's reworked version, Darvell is replaced by a character named Lord Ruthven.

Titled "The Vampyre," the story first appeared in print in the *New Monthly Magazine* in April 1819. Rather embarrassingly for Polidori, though, authorship in this case was credited to Lord Byron. Both of them attempted to set the record straight, but Henry Colburn, the commercially minded editor of the publication, clearly sensed there would be much more interest aroused in a story that was supposedly written by Byron, who was then at the height of his notoriety and fame.

Even later, when it was republished as a short book of eighty-four pages, it was once more Lord Byron who featured on the title page as the author. Only in subsequent editions was Polidori's name substituted in place of Byron's, long after the book had proved to be very popular.

The key aspect of the story was the way that it served to mark the beginning of the development of modern ideas and thoughts surrounding vampires, as was achieved through the character of Lord Ruthven. Aristocratic and wealthy, as well as possessing considerable seductive power, Ruthven was far removed from the peasant vampires that had been documented up until that stage. He was an evil, cunning, and credible individual.

The story tells how a wealthy young orphan called Aubrey meets Lord Ruthven at a society event. The pair then decide to set off on a journey around Europe, until Ruthven attempts to seduce a daughter of a friend in Rome. Being left behind, Aubrey heads to Greece, where he falls in love with the beautiful Ianthe. When they are talking, she discusses the many tales that exist about vampires in the area, causing Aubrey to realize that their characteristics could easily apply to his former traveling companion.

Tragically, Ianthe is found dead, with her throat cut and a distinctive dagger by her side. Soon afterward, Aubrey becomes ill but Ruthven returns and helps him to recover, allowing the pair to continue their trip together. En-route, however, they are brutally attacked. Ruthven is mortally wounded, but before he dies, he swears Aubrey to secrecy, saying that he must not mention either him or his past for a full year plus a day. Following his death, Aubrey is puzzled and horrified to find that the sheath of the dagger that killed Ianthe was in Ruthven's possession.

Once back in London, Aubrey settles back to life as normal, until he miraculously encounters Lord Ruthven again, seemingly in perfect health, who reminds him of his oath of silence. He then discovers that his sister is due to be married to the Earl of Marsden, who turns out to be Ruthven, thanks to the fact that he inherited an earldom. The marriage is due to take place immediately after his promise to Ruthven ends. But it then turns out that his sister is already dead, devoid of blood, and his former traveling companion has disappeared once more. Overcome with emotion, the tragedy is concluded with Aubrey's own death.

It is hard to overstate the impact that *The Vampyre* had on popular culture at the time, with the journey to Lake Geneva probably being the high point of Polidori's life. He himself saw little benefit from the success of his writing. After being fired by Byron, Polidori soon returned to life in London, following a brief period in Italy. He ended up dying in mysterious circumstances in London, just five years after that eventful trip to Switzerland, having become badly afflicted by depression and crippled by gambling debts.

Meanwhile, another lasting horror story and character emerged from that writing session on the shore of Lake Geneva. It was here that Mary Wollstonecraft Godwin created Frankenstein, in the Gothic novel *Frankenstein; or, The Modern Prometheus.*

Polidori and Mary Shelley were not the first to write about vampiric and wider horror themes, but their works helped to raise the popularity of the genre to a new level. They created a lasting demand for such stories, riven by darkness and uncertainty and often set in disturbing locations such as crypts, generating an overwhelming, unpredictable sense of discomfort, uncertainty and fear.

Another Character Emerges

While *The Vampyre* paved the way for a new perspective on vampires, our modern view of vampirism and its lead character has been shaped by a subsequent novel written in the 1890s. It is based extensively on the history and folklore of Transylvania, which represents the central region of modern-day Romania.

Written by the Irish author Bram Stoker (1847–1912), this Gothic horror novel, simply entitled *Dracula*, was published in 1897. He stumbled across this name, which has since become synonymous with vampire mythology, while staying in the English coastal town of Whitby in Yorkshire, where he worked extensively on the novel and actually set some of the scenes.

The novel opens with Jonathan Harker, who is an English solicitor, visiting Count Dracula's castle in the Carpathian Mountains. The count is a client, whom Harker is assisting to purchase a property in London. Warned not to roam the castle, Harker nevertheless ignores his host's advice and stumbles across three women, all of whom are vampires. Rescued and then abandoned in the castle by the count, who travels to Whitby, Harker ultimately follows.

Meanwhile, a friend of his soon-to-be wife, Lucy Westenra, unexpectedly falls ill, and Professor Abraham Van Heising, who is a Dutch doctor and polymath, is called in to help her. He realizes that she is the victim of a vampire, displaying the characteristic bite marks on her neck. He and his friends try to assist her by providing regular blood transfusions, although these fail to improve her condition. Van Heising advises using garlic to protect her, hanging bulbs in her room and making a garland of garlic flowers to place around her neck, along with a gold crucifix. Unfortunately, this is stolen by a maid, and Lucy's mother, unaware of the protective effect of the garlic, throws it away because of its unpleasant smell, which results in her daughter's demise.

Stoker also gave a new meaning to the description of "the un-dead" at this stage, and indeed, he seriously considering using this title for his book, rather than *Dracula*. In the context of vampires, Stoker's usage refers to the way that even after death, they continue to show traits of the living, with this having been a characteristic that was previously associated with Frankenstein.

The introduction of a female vampire into the *Dracula* story paved the way for filmmakers to cast beautiful seductive women in such roles,

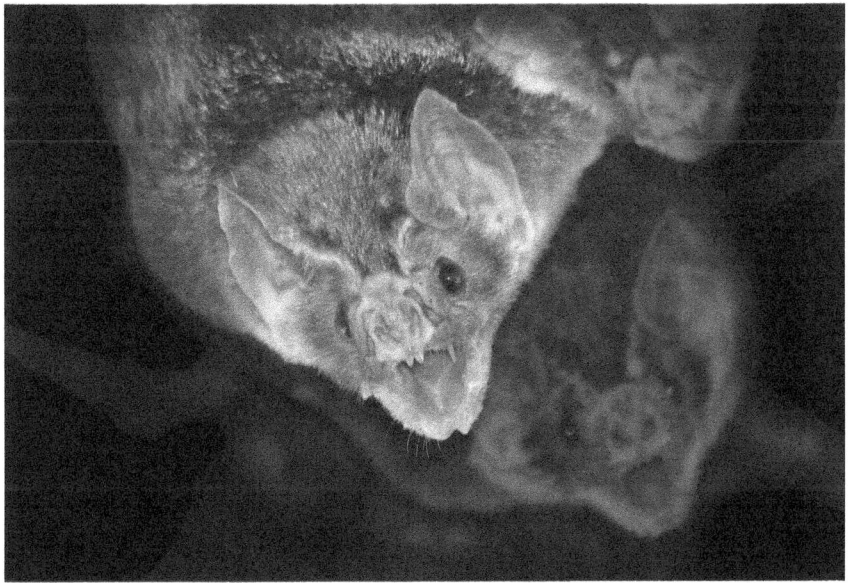

A common vampire bat.
Photo courtesy belizar/www.shutterstock.com

most notably in the Hammer Film Productions. Their 1958 movie, again simply titled *Dracula*, which starred Christopher Lee in the title role, saw the image of the fanged Dracula brought to a screen audience and subsequently etched into the public consciousness. Playing opposite Peter Cushing who had the role of Doctor Van Helsing, *Empire* magazine placed Lee's performance in 7th position, on their list of the Greatest Horror Movie Characters of All Time.

When the film was released in the North American market, however, it had to be retitled as the *Horror of Dracula* to avoid confusion with the first *Dracula* movie with sound, which had been produced in 1931 by Universal Pictures. This film about the legendary count drew on a 1924 play written by Hamilton Deane and John L. Balderston and had proved to be a big critical and commercial success.

The first actual vampire film had been released in German two years earlier and was called *Nosferatu: A Symphony of Horror*, being created by the German expressionist filmmaker F. W. Murnau (1888–1931). It was based on Stoker's *Dracula*, but some aspects were changed, although this did not prevent Stoker's widow, Florence, from suing and winning a legal action for breach of copyright against the filmmakers.

As part of its judgment, the court ordered that every copy of *Nosferatu* should be destroyed, but luckily, a single copy that had previously been screened outside Germany survived and has since been widely copied. Nowadays, the film is regarded as having been very significant in shaping the development of not just the Dracula story but actually the horror film genre in more general terms on the big screen.

In the early days of film, the special effects that could be employed were exceedingly limited, even by a leading company such as Universal Pictures, which gave their version of *Dracula* a budget of $355,050 in 1931 (equivalent to just under $6.5 million today). It starred the Hungarian actor Béla Lugosi in the lead role and was directed by Tod Browning. Evocative lighting could be used and mist replicating the appearance of fog could be created, but otherwise the possibilities were very constrained, especially when compared with the AI options that are available to filmmakers today.

Vampirism and Bats

But a lasting legacy from the film was the way that Dracula's character was able to shape-shift between a human and a bat, giving him power of flight, even though in this case, the transformation could not actually be shown occurring on-screen.

It made perfect sense to employ a bat for this purpose, though, given that, like Dracula, they are nocturnal creatures, and indeed, three living species of bat are known to feed on blood. First recognized by science in the 1820s, it is believed that vampire bats as a group first split off from the rest of the bat family around twenty-six million years ago. It has long been a puzzle as to what drew these flying mammals to feed on blood, but current thinking suggests that they probably started to hunt insects, most likely flies that were drawn to injuries where blood was present. As time passed, these bats began to evolve to feed exclusively on blood.

The oldest member of the group is the hairy-legged vampire bat (*Diphylla ecaudata*), which ranges from southern parts of Mexico down across Central America and into South America. There is a single reference to a specimen of this species being discovered in an abandoned railroad tunnel, close to Comstock in Texas, over 430 miles (700 km) from its usual range, although a further two species of vampire bat have been recognized in the fossil record from North America.

The hairy-legged vampire bat feeds predominantly on the blood of wild birds, but it may sometimes prey on domestic stock such as cattle and may even suck the blood of humans on occasion.

Vampire bats changed remarkably fast in appearance over a relatively short period of time, as they developed their blood-sucking lifestyles. In little more than about four million years, they were transformed to become the only blood-sucking mammals, with their appearance altering correspondingly. Gone was the flat area, called the nose leaf, seen attached vertically at the end of the nose, and instead, this was replaced by a much shorter, conical-shaped muzzle, enabling them to get closer into the body of their prey.

Their pattern of dentition altered to reflect their new, specialized feeding habits too. The front teeth of vampire bats are sharp and pointed, enabling them to puncture skin easily above a blood vessel, allowing them to obtain blood with relative ease. In addition, their molar teeth at the back of the mouth are significantly reduced in size, as they are not required for chewing.

Perhaps more remarkable still, however, are the methods that vampire bats have evolved to home in on their target and then feed effectively and efficiently. They possess a unique ability among mammals to seek out infrared radiation, which allows them to find a suitable food source in the dark, thanks to the animal's body heat. They also have keen hearing, which is particularly well attuned to the sound of regular breathing patterns of animals that are asleep.

Vampire bats not only possess the ability to fly but are also surprisingly agile on the ground compared with other bats. Unlike other types of mammals, where the hind legs provide the main propulsive force when running, it is the bat's forelimbs that allow them to move in this way. They have a very distinctive bounding gait as a result that allows them to move relatively safely among the feet of cattle, for example, which are likely to be bitten in a vulnerable area just above the hoof.

These bats do have a particular weakness, however, in terms of food. They will die if they are not able to consume blood within two days, and finding suitable sources for this purpose is not always easy. As a result, not only are they highly social by nature, living in colonies, but individuals will not hesitate to share their food, regurgitating liquid blood to sustain other members of the colony when required.

Out of the three species, it is the common vampire bat (*Desmodus rotundus*) that is most likely to feed on humans, although it normally preys on other mammals, particularly farm stock. As it approaches its victim the bat uses its ability to detect heat to locate where there is an accessible superficial blood vessel close to the skin. This then enables it to puncture the skin in the right place and obtain a meal as quickly as possible. If there is hair present, the bat uses its broader molar teeth in combination with the canine teeth at the corners of the mouth to cut this away. The bat will subsequently lick the site repeatedly in advance of inflicting a cut through which it can extract blood.

The actual bite, made by the incredibly sharp incisor teeth at the very front of the mouth is small, only measuring about 0.2 inch (7 mm) in width. The process is also relatively painless, which is important, as otherwise it would be impossible for the bat to feed if it disturbed the animal at the outset. Feeding is then facilitated by chemicals. A natural anticoagulant in the saliva of the common vampire bat prevents the blood from clotting as normal, which is why licking the skin is important. There are also other compounds in the saliva that prevent the blood vessels themselves from constricting and slowing blood loss. On average, a vampire bat will feed for about twenty minutes, during which it will suck up at least half its body weight of 1.4 ounces (40 g) in blood, which will be inconsequential to a large mammal like a cow.

Another link to the behavior sometimes associated with human vampires is that a number of viruses can be transmitted directly via blood. Thus viruses can be introduced to victims' bodies by the bat's feeding habits as it flies from host to host. Bats themselves, however, are resistant to their effects.

Vampire bats—and indeed other species found elsewhere in the world—can notably be a reservoir of the deadly rabies virus. In South America, it has been known for over a century that bats represent a route of infection for cattle, and the first case of a person dying from rabies following the bite of a vampire bat was documented in the 1500s.

Rabies can be a cause of sudden illness and death, although much depends on where the infected bat bites. If it does so on an extremity on the lower part of the body, it may take months for symptoms of the disease to become apparent, as the virus slowly tracks through the peripheral nerve pathways to reach the central nervous system. Death is, however, usually rapid once symptoms appear, resulting some two to ten days later. This is typically preceded by a fever, with more alarming symptoms becoming pronounced as the virus reaches the brain. These can include signs of paranoia and fear, as well as hydrophobia—fear of water—which is seen in approximately 80 percent of cases of rabies in people.

While the effects of rabies are well-recognized today, its impact in the past, with its cause unknown, would have been both distinctive and quite frightening. The person afflicted by the virus could have suffered a minor bite possibly, or simply allowed infective saliva from a dog perhaps to enter a cut. They may well have simply forgotten the incident that was to lead to their death, which may have occurred months before.

Vampires in Recent Times

From the earliest days of tales surrounding vampires, it is clear that belief in creatures of this type arose over the course of centuries from the fact that there was no true understanding of the transmission of killer infectious diseases, combined with no real appreciation of the changes that could occur to the body after death. Subsequently, though, vampires did not fade from public consciousness but gained an even wider following through books, in the first instance, followed by film.

There the story might end. But vampires still loom large in our consciousness, as shown by the unsettling case of what became known as the Highgate Vampire. The events trace back to the cemetery of this name, which opened in 1839 to accommodate a growing number of London's dead, local churchyards having become full as the population of the city had grown significantly over the years.

Highgate Cemetery soon became the final resting place of many leading names of the Victorian era and beyond, perhaps most notably Karl Marx (1818–1883), who is popularly regarded as the founder of Communism. Many of the original tombs in the cemetery were built in an elaborate Gothic style, resembling small buildings, while underground, there are also subterranean catacombs where bodies were interred in coffins placed on racks, as a means of saving space.

Although the graveyard is still used for burials today, large areas resemble a wooded park, as nature has retaken much of the land. Trees and shrubs grow over a wide area, while at ground level, ivy tumbles over a number of the tombs. Some people may view the atmosphere as serene, but undeniably, this graveyard, which has become the final resting place of some 170,000 souls, has a rather unsettling aura, especially when walking along the unmade paths on a dark, wet winter's day.

The case of the Highgate Vampire, however, began originally at the end of October 1968, in another of London's burial grounds, known as the Tottenham Park Cemetery. It was in this setting that a coffin was defiled, with a cross being driven through the lid, into the chest of the corpse below. Attention subsequently switched to the Highgate Cemetery when on Christmas Eve, 1969, a man named David Farrant claimed to have encountered what he subsequently described as a supernatural gray figure in the cemetery. He spoke with the local newspaper about this encounter and asked for anyone else who had a similar experience to get in touch. There were a variety of ghosts and disembodied voices reported both from within the cemetery and the adjacent Swain's Lane. The reports also encouraged Seán Manchester to contact the paper, claiming that what Farrant had witnessed was actually a vampire.

This was to mark the start of the development of a disagreement that ultimately escalated into a bitter feud between the two men, often played out in public through the media. It also led to an outbreak of hysteria when a mob converged at the cemetery in March 1970, just hours after television coverage of what was happening there had been broadcast, in spite of police attempts to prevent an incursion. Many of those present were said to be equipped with stakes.

Manchester and two colleagues entered a vault where they discovered three empty coffins. Salt was sprinkled over them, along with Holy Water, with garlic and a cross left in each one. Manchester has stated that he is a bishop and a UK Primate of the Old Catholic Church (which split off from Roman Catholicism during the 1870s), as well as a vampire-hunter. It is worth noting that Farrant followed the Wiccan creed, with the guiding principle of doing no harm.

In August of that year, the remains of a woman who had been dead for over a century were discovered, having been disinterred from her final resting place. She had been decapitated and burnt, having apparently been carried out from Highgate's catacombs. Some weeks later, Farrant was arrested and charged with trespass, having been found in the area in possession of a wooden stake as well as a crucifix, but the case was dismissed, on the grounds that the cemetery was a public space.

Soon after his rival's arrest, Bishop Manchester entered another vault in the graveyard, claiming that on this occasion, he had discovered a genuine vampire there. Rather than plunging a stake into the body, which would have been against the law, he resorted to carrying out an exorcism and used garlic and incense before sealing the tomb.

Farrant was then arrested again four years later and ended up facing charges of interfering with the remains of deceased persons, as well as damaging tombs in Highgate Cemetery. On this occasion, he was found guilty, in spite of claiming that it was the work of Satanists, and ended up being sentenced to jail.

Manchester reached the conclusion that a so-called King Vampire was active in Highgate, having originally stalked the area of Wallachia (now part of Romania) in medieval times, before recently being resurrected by devil worshippers in London. The remarkable story of events in the area resurfaced in 1977, when Bishop Manchester described how he had been called to a mansion near the cemetery to investigate a reported haunting. He stumbled across a coffin concealed in the basement of the property, and when he shifted the lid, he reported seeing the same King Vampire that he had encountered previously. On this occasion, Manchester admitted driving a stake into the body, which transformed into slime. He then burnt the coffin, and soon afterward the house itself was demolished.

The story, however, did not end there, as various reports of animals of different types, found dead and drained of blood, then surfaced in the area soon afterward. At this point, the story takes an even more remarkable turn. Bishop Manchester proposed that the Highgate vampire lived on in the guise of a second vampire it had created by biting someone prior to being vanquished.

He then claimed to have tracked down a woman named Lusia, buried in another cemetery in north London, who had been transformed in this way. Indeed, according to Manchester, when he visited the cemetery, he encountered a massive spider about the size of a cat and that, having driven a stake into it, it morphed back into Luisa. He then reinterred her remains.

Although that was the end of reported vampiric encounters linked with Highgate and its cemetery, the rivalry between Manchester and Farrant continued, right up until the latter's death in April 2019. They both published separate accounts about what had occurred, with Farrant proposing that the area was crossed by ley lines, which are considered by psychic researchers to be energy conduits, and this, in his view, could have allowed a vampire to manifest when conditions were favorable.

In the twenty-first century therefore, the cult of the vampire still remains powerful, drawing in people even today, in organizations such as the Atlanta Vampire Alliance. Members may be of a so-called sanguinarian (blood-drinking) disposition, drinking a few tablespoons of human blood on occasions, with appropriate permission from the donor. It is believed the life force energy present here, described as "prana," is the key ingredient of the blood for these particular modern-day vampires. The other group consists of psychic or "psi" vampires, who feed by means of direct energy transfer, from individuals or groups of people. In addition, some regard themselves as hybrid or psi/sang vampires who can draw from both energy sources.

Meanwhile, interest in vampires in films and gaming continues apace, with seemingly no end to movies in this genre. These have broadened out over time, in terms of their approach, so that although many are scary, there are comedic and even romantic variations on the theme. Television too has not been slow to appreciate the interest that exists in vampires, with probably the best known series of its type, *Buffy the Vampire Slayer*, running for 144 episodes between 1997 and 2003. The concept came from a film written by Joss Whedon, which premiered in 1992, and he subsequently developed the concept into this highly successful television series.

Adding up the number of movies with a vampire theme, more than three hundred had been produced by the turn of the century, with roughly a third featuring Dracula himself. Even more remarkably perhaps, the number of novels written about vampires has now topped a thousand.

Ten Things You May Not Know About Vampires

1 While there is no universal agreement on where the word originated, many people believe that the description of "vampire" came from an Albanian word *dhampir*. This literally means "to drink with teeth." It first appeared in an English dictionary in 1734.

2 A group of vampires may be called a brood, clutch, or pack, among other terms.

3 The blood disorder known as porphyria is sometimes described as "Vampire Disease" because of the symptoms associated with this illness. These include a dislike of sunlight and the teeth can develop a red, blood-like staining.

4 Vampires are known from other countries too. In China, they are described as "ch'ing shih" (literally meaning "corpse-hoppers"), because during the Qing dynasty (1644–1912 CE), bodies were carried on bamboo poles, making it appear as if they were bouncing along.

5 Chinese vampires are recognizable by their red eyes and crooked claws. Notorious for attacking women, they are also said to possess the ability to transform into wolves.

6 There was a belief that werewolves could sometimes become vampires, without needing to be bitten by another vampire.

7 Female vampires have been recorded. The most famous was the main character in *Carmilla*, a novella written by Joseph Sheridan Le Fanu, first published in 1872.

8 When the famous Dracula actor Béla Lugosi died in 1956, at the age of seventy-three, he was said to have been buried in his full costume, including the cape that he wore playing this role.

9 Lugosi actually turned down the role of Frankenstein, in a film based on Mary Shelley's novel, and the part went instead to British actor Boris Karloff, marking the beginning of a persistent rivalry between the pair thereafter.

10 It is thought that those with red hair were most likely to be vampires in the medieval period.

6

THE CURSE OF

WEREWOLVES AND DOGMEN

The popular modern image of a werewolf.
Photo courtesy leolintang/www.shutterstock.com

There's a frightening belief that grew up during the medieval period in Europe that has continued to this day, even being transposed further afield to the bayous of Louisiana and elsewhere. Although the name may have changed, the underlying sense of horror associated with it remains unaltered. As with the vampire, this speaks again to a deep-seated fear within the human psyche.

Early Origins

The roots of belief in lycanthropy—meaning the ability of people to change into wolves—date back even earlier, certainly to the period of ancient Greece. There are a number of such accounts, with the description originating from one of the earliest, which can be traced to the second century BCE. It involves King Lycaon of Arcadia, who was visited by the Greek god Zeus. Keen to determine whether this humble-looking man was indeed a god, Lycaon killed a prisoner and gave him part of his body to eat, according to the poet Ovid (43 BCE—17/18 CE), in the poem *Metamorphoses*. Zeus was so disgusted by what Lycaon had done that he transformed the king into a wolf. Ovid also described how in Arcadia, which is now regarded as an area of the central Peloponnese in Greece, there were men that took the form of wolves and roamed the forests there.

The belief grew in classical times that spells could be used to transform people into wolves, and this in turned was picked up by writers in the early Christian period, such as Augustine of Hippo (354–430 CE), a Berber from North Africa who is better known today as Saint Augustine. As with the Greek writer Pliny the Elder (23/24–79 CE), he described how witches could cast spells to transform people into werewolves.

This view in turn became incorporated into the *Capitulatum Episcopi*, which was the early Church's doctrinal text relating to the field of witches and transformations of people into the form of animals. It was believed that people could assume other animal identities, such as witches' ability to change (or transmogrify) into cats. The guidance in this early Christian work was very clear, however: anyone who believed that such change was possible without God's involvement was without doubt an infidel.

It is hard to overemphasize the terror associated with werewolves and how widespread this fear became at a relatively early stage in history. Gervase of Tilbury (1150–1220 CE), a cleric and advisor to Henry II of England, stated that in England, people changing into wolves was often seen. He also picked up a common thread on such transformations, originally referred to by Pliny the Elder, describing how those undergoing this change tore off their clothes beforehand.

Commemorated in Song

There is no doubt that such beliefs were commonplace right across Europe during the medieval period. In France for example, the theme featured in a well-known Breton *lai* (a short type of rhyming poem which was sung) entitled *Bisclavret*, dating to about 1200. This was written by a noblewoman under the pseudonym of Marie de France who, in addition to her own writing, also translated *Aesop's Fables* from Middle English into Anglo-Norman French. Active at the same time as Gervase of Tilbury, it is believed that she too was somehow connected to the court of Henry II, although her real name is unknown today.

This *lai* told the story about how a nobleman called Bisclavret disappeared for three days each week. Perplexed by these regular absences, his wife begs him to tell her where he goes. The baron ultimately reveals the truth: he is a werewolf, and is forced to hide his clothes until he can transform back into a person. Horrified by this disclosure, his wife looks to escape and does so by persuading a knight who is in love with her to hide her husband's clothes, forcing him to remain as a wolf. Everyone then assumes that the baron has died, leaving his wife free to marry the knight.

About a year later, when the king is out hunting with his hounds, he is amazed when a wolf comes up to him and licks his feet and legs. He orders the hounds to be taken away and decides to take the wolf back to his castle. Everyone at the king's court is amazed by the tame behavior of the wolf. Then one day, the knight who married Bisclavret's wife visits the castle for a feast, and the wolf's behavior changes dramatically. It launches into a ferocious attack on the knight. Everyone is very puzzled by this display of aggression: the only explanation appears to be that the wolf must have been harmed by the knight previously.

Soon afterward, the king sets off to visit the knight and his wife, at Bisclavret's former home, taking the wolf with him. Once again, in a reaction that seems totally out of character, the wolf viciously turns on the woman, biting her nose off. Searching for an explanation, the king consults a wise man, who explains that the only people who have been attacked by the wolf were linked to Bisclavret's disappearance, including his former wife.

The king decides to investigate further, and the woman is forced to tell the truth as to why Bisclavret vanished, after which, she is then compelled to return his clothes. Yet when the clothing is placed in front of the wolf by the king's servants, it is ignored. Puzzled by this, the king seeks further advice from his wise counsellor, who advocates placing the clothing in a room with the wolf on his own.

Soon afterward, Bisclavret himself emerges from the room, much to the king's delight. Bisclavret's lands are restored to him, and the knight and his former wife are sent into exile. As a postscript to the story, it is said that the woman's female descendants are often born without noses or are otherwise deformed.

The impact of this *lai* spread across Europe. It evolved into one of the Old Norse Chivalric sagas later in the thirteenth century, under the Norwegian title of *Bisclaretz ljóð*, featuring among the collection of tales contained in a popular compendium known as *Strengleikar*. In due course, a modified version of the story then proved to be popular in Iceland, being known there as the *Tiódels Saga*, with Tiódels assuming the role of Bisclavret in this case, although the main features of the original French version of the story remained unaltered.

Deeply Feared

It is perhaps difficult nowadays to appreciate the fear that wolves instilled in people at that stage in history. Wolves were common across most of Europe, being the most widely occurring mammal in the northern hemisphere, with their eerie howls echoing across the landscape at night. Wolves gained a ghoulish reputation in other more evident ways as well. As an example, following the Battle of Hastings in southern England, when the Normans successfully invaded from France in 1066, the dead and dying were left to the mercy of packs of wolves drawn to the carnage, which must have been a gruesome spectacle. Similar scenes played out after all major battles.

Its innate cunning and boldness made the wolf a formidable adversary: an opportunistic hunter, ready to strike even in the most unlikely surroundings. In France for example, where wolf attacks were relatively common, there is a

A wolf howling at the moon.
Photo courtesy Mongkol Rujitham/www.shutterstock.com

notorious case of a young girl who was leading a large religious procession being snatched from the street. In spite of being pursued by more than three hundred people, the wolf managed to elude them and disappeared into the forest with the child, who was never seen again.

In this case, the belief quickly spread that a werewolf must have been responsible, which led to a hunter taking his ammunition to be blessed by a priest, before setting off on his own to search for the animal. He managed to track the wolf and shot it, but this case has a tragic ending because the man was so overcome by the emotion surrounding the event that he himself also died there in the forest.

Although wolves do not normally target people as prey, there are occasions when particular wolves develop into man-eaters. This is often because they are old or in some way disabled, which makes hunting difficult for them, and people—especially children—represent relatively easy targets compared with other potential prey.

For centuries, the much feared and incurable viral disease known as rabies could also turn wolves into killers of people. The French description for this infection is *la rage*—literally meaning "the rage." When affected by this disease, a wolf will become abnormally aggressive and foams at the mouth, lunging and biting at every opportunity, making it extremely dangerous. Even if a person survived an attack by a rabid wolf, they themselves would have acquired the rabies virus through its bites, which until recently would have been a death sentence. This horrible demise would not have been instant under these circumstances either but could occur anywhere from days to years later, depending how far from the central nervous system the bite occurred, as well as the amount of virus that entered the body.

French Reports

Perhaps unsurprisingly, France was a particular center for reports of werewolves, and there were a number of trials of those accused of being werewolves. One of the most notorious took place there and involved a man named Gilles Garnier, who ultimately became known as the Werewolf of Dole. He lived in a remote home in this area, which lies within the province of Franche-Comté in the east of the country.

There was a sense of panic within the local community when children began to disappear, starting in 1572. Garnier had recently married but was finding it difficult to provide for his new wife, and they were frequently hungry. For some bizarre and sickening reason, he started killing and eating local children. Garnier was ultimately caught when seen by a group of workers who thought they had spotted a wolf, but once they got closer, they encountered him crouched over the body of a child. He was arrested, and at his trial over fifty witnesses attested to having seen him as a person and as a werewolf or *loup-garou*, to use the French description.

Confessing to the crimes of lycanthropy and witchcraft, Garner was burned at the stake in January 1574. At his trial, he explained that while out in the forest seeking food at night, he had encountered a ghost that had gifted him an ointment. He rubbed this on his body, and it allowed him to assume the appearance of a wolf, which made it easier for him to hunt.

Another similar French case of cannibalism arose slightly later, in the 1590s and involved Nicolas Damont, who became known as the Werewolf of Châlons, or the Demon Tailor of Châlons, as he lured his victims into his tailor's shop. In the guise of a werewolf, he reputedly hunted children in the forest. Damont too was ultimately sentenced to be burned to death in 1598.

Notorious Cases

However, the most notorious werewolf case from that era took place in what is now Germany, highlighting the links that were thought to exist between witchcraft, werewolves, and cannibalism. This case was so notorious at the time that a detailed account, extending over sixteen pages, was published in English, based on the original German account, which unfortunately has now been lost.

A wealthy farmer, Peter Stumpp, admitted to having used black magic since the age of twelve. He confessed to feeding on the blood of animals, as well as that of women and children. The Devil had given him a belt, which allowed him to transmogrify (or change form) into a wolf. Simply removing the belt permitted him to assume human form again. Sensationally, Stumpp described how he had left the belt in a particular valley in the area, although a thorough search could not locate it.

It is believed that Stumpp was also missing his left hand. This injury was assumed to reinforce his guilt, simply because the werewolf in question was rumored to be missing its left paw. Unsurprisingly, Stumpp was condemned to death for his crimes, being executed on October 31, 1589.

The links between werewolves and witchcraft were frequently exploited by the authorities in trials, as reflected by the case of Hans the Werewolf in the Baltic country of Livonia (which forms much of Latvia today). Hans confessed to the accusation that he was a werewolf, after his arrest in 1651. When questioned further, he explained that a man dressed entirely in black had facilitated the transformation, making the fatal mistake of confirming that when he took the form of the wolf, he felt himself to be the actual animal. The court therefore interpreted this response as confirmation that black magic was involved and this was therefore actually a case of witchcraft.

Nevertheless, it did not always prove to be possible to reach this conclusion, as in the later case of Thiess of Kaltenbrun, who was charged in 1692. A man in his eighties, Thiess readily accepted that he was a werewolf, while professing to being a hound of God. He explained how, in the company of other werewolves, he would transform for three nights each year and enter Hell, in order to battle with the Devil and his servants. Their aim was to rescue both livestock and grain stolen by witches.

All this emerged formally in court after a church robbery to which Thiess was a witness. He told the court of his previous appearance in court a decade earlier, after he had allegedly been attacked by a farmer who had broken his nose. According to Thiess, this assault had taken place in Hell, where in his werewolf form, he had encountered the local farmer, who was a witch. The man then battered him with a broomstick, resulting in his broken nose.

Thiess had been laughed out of court on that occasion, but now the judges became more interested, especially once they had confirmation that his nose had indeed been broken. He was subject to more intensive questioning, especially around his religious beliefs. Thiess had gained a reputation as a local healer in his community, both for people and their animals. However, his good work did not seem to draw on the power of God, so it was argued that Thiess was taking people away from a Christian path, which was itself a criminal offence.

Rather than condemning him to death as a werewolf, however, the judges decreed that Thiess should be flogged and banished from the area for the rest of his life. When questioned about how he and his fellow werewolves transformed themselves, Thiess explained that they simply wore wolf pelts, claiming that he had been given his by a farmer. When asked to identify his fellow werewolves, however, he modified his story, reverting back to the traditional idea that people went on their own into the forest and undressed, and this led directly to their transformation.

Warrior Shamans

Thiess's case raises a number of interesting points, effectively linking back to a pre-Christian tradition, where a shaman (someone who links the everyday world with the spirit world) might wear a wolf pelt. This not only could disguise the person's identity but was also believed to transfer the strength of the animal at the same time. Warrior shamans of the Viking era, which extended from about 800 to 1050 CE, were divided into two groups: the *berserkir* (literally meaning "bear shirts") and the *úlfheðnar* (pronounced "oolv-heth-nahr"), which is a word derived from the old Norse and translates as "wolf hides."

The main difference between these two groups was simply the totemic animal that inspired them. The famed Norse ruler Odin is closely linked to these so-called "warrior-shamans" who forewent any armor and would fight clad only in the skins of bears or wolves. These warriors were greatly feared on the battlefield, and their legacy is still reflected by the English phrase still used today, "going berserk," which has come to mean losing control and acting wildly.

A central part of the shamanic tradition involves letting go of the past, followed by rebirth in a different form. In the case of the *úlfheðnar*, they were compelled to undergo a state known as *raptor vivre*, which meant effectively abandoning their normal life and adopting that of a wolf living in the wild for a period, providing them with a different insight into the world. It is now unknown as to exactly what methods may have been used in assisting them in reaching this state.

Fasting probably played a part, along with exposure to the elements and possibly consuming various plants that can have medicinal properties. It meant that when they entered the battle, these warriors were totally subsumed into the identity of a wolf, wearing the skin of the animal and howling in a similar manner. In a trance-like state, hardened and shaped by their time living in the wild and probably buoyed by plant-based hallucinatory drugs, they would have appeared truly terrifying. The *Ynglinga Saga* refers both to their strength and how neither iron nor fire affected them as they killed their opponents, throwing aside their protective shields, seemingly immune to pain.

It is easy to see how accounts of such fearsome animalistic warriors, when passed down through the generations, would have played a part in maintaining an ongoing belief in werewolves for many centuries after the end of the Viking Era. Yet, gradually, beliefs began to change across Europe. King

James I (1566–1625) was among the earliest to decree those who considered themselves to be werewolves as deluded, being afflicted instead by melancholia.

The Beast of Gévaudan

In the Vaud region of Switzerland, a pastor writing in 1653 highlighted the growing view by this stage that people claiming to be werewolves were delusional. Indeed, by this stage, in France itself, where there had been a strong belief in lycanthropy, this had largely vanished. Such change might be linked to some degree to the Age of Enlightenment, which marked a new, rational and more scientific approach to life generally. Whatever the reason, the *Encyclopédie*, a work in twenty-eight volumes which was the first major reference work of its kind in French, published between 1751 and 1772, listed lycanthropy as being a mental disorder.

That this belief held was remarkable, given that one of the worst attacks, believed to have been carried out by a single wolf, took place in the country between 1764 and 1767. The Beast of Gévaudan roamed this province in France (now represented by the department of Lozère and part of Haute-Loire), striking terror in the local population because of its murderous behavior. It is believed to have carried out more than 200 attacks, within a relatively confined area of 56 × 50 miles (90 × 80 km).

It would have been very easy for lycanthropy to be blamed in this case, especially as some people claimed that the beast could walk by standing up on its hind legs. It was also said to be unaffected on occasions after being shot, suggesting a supernatural link. The situation became so bad that troops were sent to the area to track and kill this rogue wolf, followed by professional wolf hunters accompanied by specially trained bloodhounds with the aim of tracking its scent and locating it. The hunters killed a number of wolves, believing that one of them must have been responsible, but still the attacks continued unabated.

Frustrated and somewhat embarrassed by these events, King Louis XV then dispatched Lieutenant of the Hunt François Antoine to the region in 1765. In September of that year, he managed to kill a large wolf close to the Abbaye des

Chases. Some survivors identified this individual as the wolf that had attacked them, and so with great ceremony, the wolf was taken by François Antoine's son to Paris. He had it stuffed en route and it was placed on display at the king's palace at Versailles. Meanwhile, the wolf's mate and pups were hunted down and killed. Hailed as a hero, Antoine traveled back to Paris in November, convinced that his work in Gévaudan was complete.

Indeed, no further attacks were reported that month. Unfortunately, however, the start of December saw more people attacked by wolves, and the king subsequently ignored pleas for further assistance as attacks continued in the early months of 1766. Nothing seemed to work, and also, it appeared that the wolf responsible was being more wary and evasive. The breakthrough finally came on June 19, 1767, when a local man, Jean Chastel, shot and killed the animal on the slopes of La Sogne d'Auvers. Its body was subsequently examined by a surgeon named Dr. Boulanger. He concluded that it was simply a large wolf.

There is then some confusion as to what happened subsequently. It is popularly believed that the remains were again taken to Paris, while the king, who was absent at that stage, arranged for the well-known French naturalist Georges-Louis Leclerc, Comte de Buffon (1707–1788) to examine the remains. He too apparently concluded it was a large wolf, although there is no surviving evidence to this effect. The main thing for the people of Gévaudan, however, was that there were no further attacks.

The widespread availability of guns led to a major decline in the number of wolves in Europe, but in some more remote parts of the continent, such as the Austrian Alps, fear of werewolves lingered later into the century. The defense of being a werewolf was seemingly last used in Europe in 1853 by a Spanish murderer, but it was disregarded by the court.

The Silver Bullet

An interesting postscript to the Beast of Gévaudan story, however, stems from reworkings of the story in fiction, which have now become intermingled with the facts surrounding the case. The belief arose that werewolves could be killed by weapons made of silver, which stems from an incident that occurred about 1640 in the city of Greifswald, when it was reputedly being plagued by werewolves. The suggestion was made that the townsfolk needed to gather whatever silver they had, such as buttons or belt buckles, and melt these down to be made into silver bullets, which would be effective in killing the werewolves. This has given rise to the term *silver bullet* to mean a simple solution to any long-standing problem.

In the context of the Beast of Gévaudan, it is often said nowadays that it was killed with a silver bullet, but in fact, this is a much later addition to the story. This piece of information was added to accounts published from 1935 onward. In fact, a surprising number of contemporary beliefs about werewolves are modern in origin. One of the best known is the suggestion that a full moon triggers their transformation, which arose in the twentieth century and was first featured in the 1943 movie *Frankenstein Meets the Wolf Man*.

There are also fictional links between vampires and werewolves in the novel *Dracula*, by Bram Stoker, published in 1897. Here Count Dracula possesses the power to shape-shift into a wolf, thanks to his Székely heritage in Transylvania, although he can only do so under cover of darkness, unless the clock strikes noon. In the accompanying short story, called "Dracula's Guest," soldiers on horseback pursue Dracula (portrayed not as a vampire in this case but rather as a giant wolf), and describe how a special magical bullet would be needed to kill the monstrous creature.

Events in North America

While in Europe today, tales of encounters with werewolves have faded away totally, the situation is very different elsewhere in the world, notably in North America. In the early days of settlement, it was not just the English who moved to the continent but people from other European countries too. The French occupied a large swathe of territory, extending from eastern Canada in a southwesterly direction down to Louisiana and the Gulf of Mexico, giving rise to the Cajun culture that exists in the area today. Aside from their language, these early settlers also brought stories from their homeland, including accounts of werewolf-like animals in various forms.

Today, the traditional French word *loup-garou*, literally meaning "werewolf," has morphed in Louisiana into *rougarou*. This is the most common spelling, although there are other local variants such as "rugaroo" and "rugaru." Cajun culture in the area describes the rougarou's appearance as combining the head of a wolf with a human body.

It was said that any Catholics who failed to follow the rules of the religious festival of Lent, prior to Easter, would be targeted and killed by the rougarou. This seemingly links back to the original French story that if Catholics failed to follow the rules surrounding Lent for seven years, they would be transformed into a loup-garou.

Other tales surrounding the rougarou developed in Louisiana, including direct links to the occult. If a witch shape-shifted to become a wolf herself, she could then create rougarous, simply by cursing people. There was a widespread belief that rougarous themselves could then directly infect other people, by sucking their blood.

Affected individuals would be transformed into werewolves during the hours of darkness and then regain human form at dawn. They remained in this state for 101 days, with a full moon encouraging rougarous to start wandering across the land, in search of victims. During the day, although they would revert to human form, those who were rougarous would appear to be sick but would not reveal the cause of their affliction.

Stories of the rougarou are still widespread in Louisiana even today, with many local variants being told, reflecting the situation that often occurs in the case of a long-standing oral tradition. It is sometimes said that such accounts were developed as a way of keeping children safe, deterring them from wandering off, in areas where not only wolves but other potentially lethal predators, notably venomous snakes, bears, pumas (*Puma concolor*), and American alligators (*Alligator mississippensis*), could lurk and strike unexpectedly. Raising children there would have been much more dangerous for the early generations of French settlers than would have been the case in Europe. Older residents in particular still talk about the fear that they remember as children, when their parents told them tales of the rougarou.

The Case of the Chupacabra

The chupacabra, which is pronounced "choo·puh·kaa·bruh," is a relatively new addition to reports of mysterious canid-like creatures from the New World. In this case, early reports came from the Caribbean island of Puerto Rico, with a puzzling series of deaths among farm stock in 1975, but it was not until two decades later that the chupacabra was formally named and blamed for these stock deaths, rather than a Satanic cult.

A key feature linked with such attacks are the small circular holes left on the bodies of the attacked animals through which blood is thought to be drained from the body. The description of "chupacabra" come from a combination of two Spanish words, with *chupa* meaning "sucks" and *cabras* translating as "goats," which are often its reputed victims. It was a well-known Puerto Rican DJ named Silverio Pérez, who named the creature live on-air.

Descriptions of the chupacabra suggest the creatures are bipedal, about the size of a small bear, with large eyes and spines running from its head down along its back, creating a rather reptilian appearance. Other features included hairless bodies and sharp claws. This description is closely linked to that given by a witness named Madelyne Tolentino, who claimed to have seen one of these creatures in August 1995, close to the town of Canóvanas in the northeast of the island, when about 150 animals of all types were mysteriously killed.

On closer investigation, however, Benjamin Radford, who spent five years researching the mystery, concluded that this characterization was unreliable. This was because Tolentino's description corresponds very closely to the appearance of Sil, a character in the sci-fi movie *Species*, which was released that year, and she admitted seeing this film just before describing the mysterious chupacabra.

Indeed, it seems that the case of the Puerto Rican chupacabra could have been a case of mass hysteria in certain respects. As the number of accounts mounted, it appeared animals that were simply found unexpectedly dead were now grouped as being among the chupacabra's latest victims. Significantly, no DNA tests, which might have provided an insight into the identity of the chupacabra, were undertaken, and furthermore, when

Dr. David Morales, a veterinarian with the Puerto Rican Department of Agriculture, examined three hundred supposed victims of the creature, he found that none had been exsanguinated, with all of them still having blood in their bodies.

The Chupacabra in the United States

Subsequently though, reports of chupacabras have started to come from the United States, and eyewitness accounts describe these creatures as having a much more dog-like appearance. There is no crest of reptilian spines, or huge eyes. They also walk on all fours, rather than reputedly being bipedal. A range of sightings have come from Texas, particularly in open countryside areas around San Antonio and Austin, as well as Dallas.

These triggered a spate of movies featuring so-called chupacabras, released in the first decade of the current century. They included *A Mexican Werewolf in Texas*, which sought to match the popularity of *An American Werewolf in London*, released in 1981, with the reference to a werewolf in its title but featuring what was described as a chupacabra instead. Although these films were fictional creations, they served to raise the profile of this mysterious creature, aided by the concurrent proliferation of the internet.

The name *chupacabra*, combined with its supposed vampiric tendencies, meant that it was not easily overlooked. What was very clear, however, was that the form of creature reported on the American mainland was very different from that which had generated interest originally on Puerto Rico. The similarity, in so far as there may be a link, relates to the way that some of the animals died, displaying puncture wounds on the neck.

Yet it is known that a number of predators, particularly cats, have long, sharp canine teeth at the corners of their jaws, with which they seize prey. Cats will frequently attack the neck of their prey, seizing it in their jaws and effectively suffocating it. This is a much safer method for an animal hunting on its own and tackling prey that may be of similar size, rather than grabbing it from behind and risking a fatal kick as a result.

More Insight from Texas

As in the case of many mysteries of this type, there is unfortunately a lack of evidence, not to mention consistent features in reports from Puerto Rico. But the situation is different in Texas, although there is no direct link between the chupacabra sightings in these two areas. In fact, it seems likely that the events in the Lone Star State had a different cause from those in Puerto Rico. The first sighting in Texas was reported in June 2007, when a rancher by the name of Phylis Canion spotted a strange dog-type creature on her land near Cuero, in the south-central area of the state. It was bluish-gray in appearance, with evidently bony limbs. This indicates that it could comply with the biological parameter known as Gloger's Rule, which suggests that in the case of wide-ranging species, those found closer to the equator generally have darker skin than those occurring in polar areas.

Soon afterward, Canion discovered one of her chickens had been killed, having its throat ripped apart—seemingly without any blood left in its body. Believing that the mysterious creature she had seen was responsible, she set up various cameras around her property in the hope of capturing it on film. She also reached out to her neighbors to see if they had made any sightings, experienced similar happenings, or possibly might even have shot the creature. Not long afterward, in mid-July that year, she was contacted by a fellow rancher in the area, who told her that an animal corresponding to her description had been killed by a vehicle on a road near his property.

Phylis Canion rushed to the location and was able to retrieve its body. It looked just as she had observed it previously, and samples were taken for DNA testing, in the hope of being able to establish its identity. The results, both in this case and from the examination of other supposed chupacabra remains found in Texas, have been consistent. They have revealed the corpses as being of canids: either coyotes (*Canis latrans*), a smaller relative of the wolf, or domestic dogs.

Obviously, however, something sets these specimens apart in terms of their appearance from typical examples of their type, not least in their lack of hair. A hairless gene is well-recognized in the domestic dog population in this part of the United States and farther south. A number of historic hairless breeds—

some of which have become extinct—were kept by local Native Americans, of which the best-known example today is probably the Xoloitzcuintle, being named after the Aztec god Xolotl, who was portrayed with the head of a dog and the body of a person.

A feature linked with hairlessness in dogs can often be a reduction in the number of teeth, as well as more general dental abnormalities. These are both features that have been recorded in the case of the Texan chupacabra, suggesting an underlying genetic cause. As such dogs have been kept for millennia in that area of the Americas, it is tempting to suggest that at some stage in the past, localized cross-breeding may have taken place, introducing the hairless gene into the coyote population.

The initial thought about the Texan chupacabras was, however, that such individuals were ill, potentially suffering from the disease known as mange, which is caused by parasitic mites. This leads to an affected animal—whether a domestic dog or coyote—losing its fur if the condition is left untreated. The mites can be easily transferred by close proximity to an infected individual, as would occur in a breeding den, where pups are together with their mother, providing the ideal conditions for these tiny parasites to transfer to new hosts. Strangely, it appears that no tests for mange were carried out on the bodies of the chupacabras that have been found in Texas, but certainly the mounted specimen of Phylis Canion's example shows no evident signs of mange.

There are two forms of mange. The sarcoptic form (*Sarcoptes scabiei*) is very irritating and will cause a dog to scratch itself repeatedly, to the extent that if untreated, it is likely to cause self-inflicted injuries. Demodectic mange tends to be much rarer and more localized in its effects on the body, although if generalized, it becomes very itchy, and the resulting injuries often show signs of bacterial infection.

Although some suspected chupacabras may be suffering from mange, the total absence of fur over the entire body and lack of self-inflicted injuries, combined with dental abnormalities (which are not induced by this disease) are more suggestive of a genetic explanation. This would appear to be borne out by tests carried out on the bodies of three US chupacabras, with two diagnosed as suffering from mange, whereas the other displayed no signs of this illness.

Under these circumstances, the relatively infrequent sightings of supposed Texan chupacabras are simply a reflection of the fact that the genes responsible are not widely distributed through the coyote or feral dog populations in the area. Confirming that canids of the area do hybridize, the study of another Texan chupacabra, dubbed the Blanco Texas Chupacabra, revealed it to be the result of cross-breeding between a coyote and the Mexican subspecies of the wolf.

No Single Solution

This explanation could not apply in the Puerto Rican cases, however, simply because there are no coyotes present there and no known hairless breed of dog. As there is only one sighting on record, with a description based on a film character, but many more cases where the involvement of a chupacabra has been suspected, it is quite possible that ordinary stray dogs may explain the deaths. Their canine teeth can create the puncture marks described on the bodies of the animals.

The image of the chupacabra remains strong in the public's mind, however, to the extent that sightings attributed to the beast have now been recorded from a wide area of the world, with the northeastern parts of the United States being another chupacabra hot spot. Further reports from Mexico, Nicaragua, and down to Chile have been made, and elsewhere in the world, the Philippines and India are countries that now have accounts of chupacabra-like creatures in their mythologies.

Dogmen

In other US areas, recent tales have appeared of what in Europe would be known as werewolves but which in the United States are better known as dogmen. Up near the Great Lakes, for example, there are accounts of the Michigan Dogman, said to occur in Wexford County, where it has been seen in the vicinity of the Manistee River. Although part of the folklore of the Odawa Native American tribes seemingly for centuries, it remained unknown to most

Americans up until 1887. In that year, two lumberjacks working in the forest in Wexford County told of their encounter with a creature they described as having the head of a dog and the body of a person.

Early Beginnings

Strangely, this is a very widespread and long-standing historical phenomenon, being recognized under the name of *cynocephaly*, which literally means "dog head." The Egyptian god Anubis, dating back to about 3100 BCE, who acted as a guide to the underworld and as a protector of graves, was portrayed with the head of either a dog or jackal and the body of a person. The ancient Greeks subsequently believed that it was the form of the head of such creatures that revealed their true origins.

There are also a number of accounts of dog-headed tribes found in India, according to various Greek writers such as Ctesias, who also described unicorns (see Chapter 1). Subsequently, in the third century BCE, an explorer named Megasthenes revealed how these tribes inhabited the mountainous region there. They dressed in animal skins and did not speak as such but communicated with each other through barking. This view was reinforced slightly later by Claudius Aelianus.

Images of cynocephali were even transposed into Christianity. Mercurius Abu-Sayfain, an early second-century saint of the Coptic Christians, a group that occupied an area equivalent to modern day Egypt and Sudan, was served by Ahrakas and Augani, also recognized as saints, who were characterized as having the heads of dogs.

St. Christopher has been portrayed in some icons of the Eastern Orthodox Church in a similar form. It is possible that this occurred initially because of a simple translation error, involving the Latin word "Cananeus," which actually means a Canaanite but may have been misinterpreted as "caninus," meaning "dog-like."

Thanks to the reliance at that stage in history on iconography, this image became established over the course of centuries. Walter of Speyer (967–1027 CE), a German bishop as well as poet, told how St. Christopher was a giant member of a tribe that communicated by barking and fed on human flesh. Later he converted to Christianity, losing his cynocephalic appearance as a result, and devoted himself to pursuing Christian ideals. In the eighteenth century, the Russian Orthodox Church took steps to ban the portrayal of St. Christopher as having the head of a dog. Similar stories also circulated around other significant figures in the early medieval world, such as St. Andrew.

In Europe at this stage, there was also debate among theologians as to whether these dog-headed creatures were human. This mattered because it was believed that only human beings had souls. It was therefore a wasted effort to preach to cynocephali if they were simply animals. There are also a number of references to them in contemporary works of the period, including the epic Anglo-Saxon poem *Beowulf*, where they are described as *healfhundingas*, translating today as "half dogs." The Welsh poem *Pa gur?* describes them as *cinbin*, meaning "dogheads," and describes a major battle with King Arthur where the great warrior Bedivere is said to have killed hundreds of these cynocephali on his own.

Travelers' Accounts

A number of European travelers visiting foreign lands returned with stories of encounters with dog-headed people. The Italian Catholic archbishop and explorer Giovanni da Pian del Carpine (c. 1185–1252) traveled to Mongolia, as the representative of Pope Innocent IV, covering an estimated 3,000 miles (4,830 km) in just 106 days on horseback. He described how the armies of Ögedei Khan had encountered a settlement of dog-headed people in an area north of Dalai-Nor, translating as the Northern Ocean, which is now known as Lake Baikal, lying in southern Siberia.

Another Asiatic traveler of this period, who has been mentioned before, is Marco Polo (see Chapter 1). He refers to a population of cynocephali whose heads resembled those of large mastiff-type dogs who lived on Angamanain (known as the Andaman Islands today), lying off the coast of India. Here they reportedly cultivated spices. Dog-headed men were also described from this part of the world in the book entitled *The Voyage and Travels of Sir John*

Mandeville, reputedly being resident nearby on the Nacumera (Nicobar Islands). This work, purportedly written between 1357 and 1371, is something of a mystery, however, being supposedly written by an English knight, although the author's precise identity is unclear.

It is interesting that accounts of dog-headed people were also recorded from the New World at a very early stage. Christopher Columbus (1451–1506) whose voyage of discovery in 1492 opened the way for European contact with the Americas, documented how the native Taino people of the Caribbean were aware of the existence of dog-headed men. The Ottoman cartographer and explorer Piri Reis (c. 1470–1553) included a drawing of a fight between a cynocephalus and a monkey, upon the country of Colombia on a map of South America that he drew for Sultan Selim I. Two years later, in 1519, the Spanish conquistador Hernán Cortés was charged by the governor of Cuba to investigate reports of these dog-headed men, collaborating the belief that they existed there.

There is a different variation on this theme in the far north, incorporated into Inuit mythology, which is particularly prevalent around Hudson Bay, as well as in the Canadian province of Labrador, extending across to Greenland. Members of the Adlet tribe were believed to have the head and body of a person, combined with the legs of a dog. Reputedly tall in stature, they could run fast as a result and supposedly often fought with humans.

The Beast of Bray Road

A twentieth-century addition to the list of Dogman-like creatures has been dubbed the Beast of Bray Road and has become firmly established as part of the folklore of the state of Wisconsin. The earliest reported encounter with this wolf-headed creature dates back to 1936. Subsequent sightings, which became much more frequent from the late 1980s into the 1990s, have remained surprisingly localized. They have taken place largely in the vicinity of Elkhorn, which is a town lying about 40 miles (64 km) southwest of Milwaukee, with the creature being named after the isolated farm road where the vast majority of encounters occurred.

Around 1991, the local newspaper, the *Walworth County Week*, became interested in the story and sent reporter Linda Godfrey to investigate the reports. It was she who coined the description "The Beast of Bray Road." Although an initial skeptic, she soon became convinced by what witnesses told her, having accumulated reports of over two dozen encounters.

A composite overview of the creature suggests that it ranges in height from 6 to 7 feet (1.8–2.1 m), according to their testimonies. Its head is said to be like that of a wolf, distinguished by the reddish-orange glow evident in its eyes, which reflect the light of car headlamps. The body has been likened to that of a person in appearance but is described as being covered in very long, shaggy hair and able to move either on two or four legs.

There are several cases of drivers claiming that they struck an animal after dark while driving along Bray Road, and in one case, having stopped, the driver was chased back into her vehicle by the creature. Scratch marks left by its claws were visible on the rear door.

Sightings have been made not just at night but during the day as well. Several witnesses have described a large, wolf-like creature running through nearby fields, seemingly chasing deer in at least one case. It seems to become more conspicuous in the fall, being able to utilize cover in cornfields at this stage. The remains of large prey have been recorded in the area, not fully eaten but with the bodies ripped apart and organs removed.

Reports have diminished over recent years, although two sightings were recorded in 2018 and 2020. The question remains as to what the Beast of Bray Road might have been, assuming it no longer survives. There have been no sightings of more than one individual, so a breeding population seems unlikely. Could it have been an abnormally large wolf, as certain observers believe? It is worth pointing out that wolves are not common in Wisconsin generally but can be seen occasionally in the area. This means, of course, that people are likely to be less familiar with them there, compared with other areas where wolves are observed more frequently, causing them to be more fearful when an encounter unexpectedly occurs.

Some eyewitnesses describe the Beast of Bray Road as having the head of a German Shepherd (Alsatian) type of dog. It could obviously have been that a stray dog had reverted to living and hunting in the wild. This would explain why the creature apparently displays little fear of people, and its long, matted coat would simply be a sign of neglect. Perhaps rather than a German Shepherd Dog, though, a more likely candidate could be its Belgian relative, known as the Teruveren, with its decidedly wolf-like face and longer coat. No single dog or wolf, however, could have a lifespan extending over the period that sightings of the Beast of Bray Road have been recorded, which adds up to more than eighty years.

This also applies to the suggestion that such sightings could be attributed to the presence of a bear in the area. More than one individual would have to have been involved. As in the case of wolves, American black bears (*Ursus americanus*), which are the smallest species present on the continent, can sometimes be seen in Walworth County. While most people encountering a bear close-up along a road would be able to identify it generally, even at night, the situation might be very different if it had been afflicted by mange. This would result in hair loss, effectively transforming its appearance, while, in a weakened state, it might be more likely to forage for roadkill for example, rather than actively hunting. While large dogs or wolves can support themselves on their hind legs for short periods, a bear is certainly more adept at standing in this way, while also being able to run at speed as a quadruped. The reported scratches on the door of a vehicle are much more the type of behavior associated with bears than any type of dog—wild or domesticated.

The period of sightings tends to suggest repeated encounters with a single individual. This could explain why sightings ceased largely within a decade, covering the lifespan of a wolf, dog, or bear. It is possible that once the original animal died, then subsequent infrequent sightings had another explanation, such as a passing sighting of a bear. As with many other cases of its type, the possibility has to be that the Beast of Bray Road could have a variety of explanations.

In Conclusion

In the case of werewolves and dogmen, what is clear is that in all cases, there is a particularly deep-seated fear of such creatures within the human psyche, extending right back to the dawn of recorded time. Few animals have been as feared throughout history as wolves, and the concept of what is effectively a human-wolf hybrid is even more terrifying. The nocturnal nature of werewolves adds to the level of fear associated with them, mirroring that of the wolf itself.

Undiagnosed psychological and medical conditions could undoubtedly help to explain cases of human werewolves like that of Peter Stumpp. The deadly viral infection known as rabies may have played a role too, with aggressive, unprovoked attacks by rabid wolves reinforcing the image of werewolves in public consciousness. The recent reported cases of chupacabra sightings reveal just how, as a species, we have altered surprisingly little in our fears, in spite of a lack of real evidence that an unrecognized creature of this type exists.

Ten Things You May Not Know About Werewolves

1   There is now a rare psychiatric condition known as clinical lycanthropy, describing a patient who is convinced they can change or shape-shift into other animals, including wolves or dogs.

2   One of the earliest attempts to recognize the symptoms of being a werewolf was made in 1563 by Johann Weyer who was a Lutheran physician. He observed that they were pale in color, with sunken, dim eyes and were usually thirsty with a dry tongue.

3   Actual symptoms of those suffering from clinical lycanthropy can include not only aggression but also wolf-like behaviors, such as howling and moving on all four limbs, accompanied by the delusion of transforming into a werewolf. Cases still occur today, but cures can now be achieved using antipsychotic medication.

4   The condition known as hypertrichosis which results in excessive growth of body hair has also been linked with lycanthropy. Excessive growth of hair on the hands in particular was believed to be a means of recognizing people who were actually werewolves in disguise.

5   A werewolf test was used in parts of France during the medieval period. It involved a yellowish fungus known as witches' butter (*Tremella mesenterica*), which has a loose jelly-like texture. If this jelly dissolved when placed on a wound, it indicated a werewolf.

6 There was a real fear in parts of Italy and France that if the groom spotted a wolf on the night of his wedding, he would become a werewolf. Families therefore went to great efforts to ensure that this did not happen, undertaking patrols to deter any wolves. Brides would use herbs to ward off any encounters too.

7 In southern parts of South America, there is a mythical wolf-like creature known as the Lobizon, with the seventh-born son in a family being likely to transform into this type of werewolf and being condemned to stalk the countryside at night for ever.

8 Canid shapeshifters in Asia are more likely to be represented by foxes. In China, the Huli jing are said to take a variety of forms, although they could often transform into beautiful women and in turn would seduce intelligent men, allowing them to remain in human form.

9 The herb called wolfsbane (*Aconitum* species) is closely associated with werewolves. It was first used by the ancient Greeks on account of its toxicity, as a way of baiting food to kill wolves. In the 1980s, a leading producer of werewolf movies at the time used the name Aconito Films for his company.

10 In the novel *Harry Potter and the Prisoner of Azkaban* by J. K. Rowling, the character Professor Snape chooses to make a potion using wolfsbanc as a way of combating the effects of lycanthropy if taken in advance of the full moon.

7

SEARCHING FOR SASQUATCH (BIGFOOT)

Typical sighting of a Sasquatch in a forested area.
Photo courtesy Fsendek/www.shutterstock.com

Native American accounts describing these giants of the woods, which reputedly stand approximately 8 feet (2.4 m) in height and weigh an estimated 900 pounds (408 kg), date back many centuries. Although there have been reports of sightings of such creatures over much of the United States, the majority are linked to the Pacific Northwest, in an area extending from British Columbia southward to California. Indeed, it was here that they acquired the description of "Sasquatch." This name derives from the language of the coastal Salish people who referred to them as *sásq'ets*, meaning "wild men," long before the arrival of European settlers in the region. There is a significant difference between the way that Indigenous Americans in the northwest view Sasquatch as being a physical living creature, compared with tribes elsewhere on the continent, particularly east of the Rocky Mountains. They tend to treat Sasquatch as more of a spirit being, credited with the power to shape-shift into a coyote (*Canis latrans*) according to some accounts.

Early Spanish explorers in North America referred to Sasquatches as "los Vigilantes Oscuros" (translating as "dark watchers"), because they reputedly crept around their camps at night. Local newspaper accounts of sightings and encounters can be traced back to 1818, and by the 1840s, reports about the "wild man of the woods," as the Sasquatch were described by this stage, were by then widespread through settler communities in the region and further

Warning notice suggesting Bigfoot is in the area.
Photo courtesy CineBlade/www.shutterstock.com

afield. As demand for timber grew significantly, and logging extended over a wider range, such encounters unsurprisingly became more numerous, and this trend shows no sign of abating.

Logging may no longer be the industry that it was, but outdoor pursuits such as hiking are drawing more people out into the woods, and a dedicated cadre of Sasquatch enthusiasts regularly head out into the wilds in search of these mysterious creatures. There have been over ten thousand recorded sightings of Sasquatches in the continental United States alone over the past fifty years. What is particularly interesting, when dividing these sightings down, is that the main areas for reports are consistently located in the Pacific Northwest, notably in Washington State, and also in Florida.

Attitudes to People

Sasquatches are believed to avoid human contact whenever possible, and even on occasions when they are reportedly spotted, they rapidly disappear into the forest, so that actual sightings are usually very brief. In the vast majority of cases, encounters with Sasquatches are peaceful, although a notable exception is said to have occurred in July 1924. In a steep-sided area close to Mount St. Helens in Washington State, now known as Ape Canyon, a group of gold prospectors had constructed a cabin that attracted the attention of local Sasquatches. According to the story, a member of the group made the mistake of shooting at one of these creatures and believed that he had wounded it. Another was apparently hit by gunfire and was seen falling off the steep slope into the gorge below. On that night, however, the men found themselves under attack from other Sasquatches, who hurled rocks and boulders at their cabin under cover of darkness. The building sustained damage, and one of the prospectors was knocked unconscious. The men were so scared by this onslaught that they left the area as soon as they could the next morning.

Stories of Sasquatch sightings in the region were common even before this event, and it was in the same area that an even more remarkable tale emerged later that century, in 1980. Mount St. Helens had been thought to be a dormant volcano, but on May 18 of that year, it erupted very violently, ranking as the deadliest volcanic event in US history. Fifty-seven people in the vicinity lost their lives, along with countless animals. Among the casualties were said to be a number of Sasquatches that were reputedly either killed or injured. It is said that government officials helped treat some of those that survived, although unsurprisingly, there is no hard evidence to this effect. As with so many stories involving these mysterious hominids, it cannot be substantiated, although interestingly, the US Army Corps of Engineers had previously included Sasquatch on its list of native species within its *Environmental Atlas for Washington*, including a map of recorded tracks and sightings prior to and after 1968.

A New Name Evolves

There are numerous casts and photographs of large footprints linked to these mysterious creatures. With a growing number of reports of this type during the second half of the twentieth century, the description of "Bigfoot" came into existence, and that has now become the popular name for these creatures. This was largely thanks to Andrew Genzoli, a reporter who wrote for the *Humboldt Times* newspaper. He was contacted by Jerry Crew, a member of a logging team working in the Six Rivers National Forest, in Humboldt County, California. Crew had spotted a series of gigantic, human-like footprints where he was working. They measured approximately 16 inches (41 cm) long, dwarfing those of any person. When Crew pointed them out to some of his fellow workers, they confirmed that they had seen similar impressions in the area too.

Genzoli was intrigued by these accounts and wrote a story that featured Crew on the front page, holding a plaster cast of one of the footprints that he had spotted. The story, which appeared on October 6, 1958, was then picked up by the national media, along with the description of "Bigfoot" as the name of the creature responsible for them.

Hoaxes—sometimes quite elaborate ones—pervade the entire field of Sasquatch research, however, extending back for more than a century, and once again, things ultimately turned out to be not exactly what they seemed in this particular case. Fast forward to 2002, when the family of

Ray Wallace, a coworker of Crew, was clearing out his property after his death. They discovered a number of large carved wooden feet concealed in his basement. It then emerged that unbeknown to his colleagues, Wallace had created the tracks with the intention of deterring any thieves who might have otherwise been tempted to take any of the items that were being used in this remote locality.

It also emerged that this was not the first occasion that this type of hoax had been carried out. Back in the 1930s, a group of woodsmen led by Rant Mullens, who was a friend of Wallace's, had used a similar method to deter pickers of wild huckleberries in the nearby Gifford Pinchot National Forest.

Even so, such cases of fakery certainly do not disprove that among the many other reputed footprints of Bigfoot, some represent genuine encounters. The depth of the impression can be particularly significant, reflecting the great weight of the creature compared with that of a human. Furthermore, tracks in some cases extend for considerable distances, making it difficult to fake them consistently, although this obviously depends to some extent on the state of the landscape. Ridges on the skin—which were missing in the case of Wallace's hoax—are also regarded as a significant detail by researchers today.

The late Dr. Grover Krantz (1931–2002) studied many supposed Bigfoot tracks and the casts taken from them. His records reveal that the average length of a cast is about 17 inches (42.5 cm), with the anatomical structure of the feet reflecting the bulk of the creatures. The arches of the feet are absent in all but perhaps younger, smaller Sasquatches, which have a lighter build, giving the majority a flat-footed walk.

Krantz, who was an anthropologist, first became interested in this area of research in 1963, and although a skeptic at first, he altered his view when he studied what became known as the Cripplefoot tracks. As their name suggests, it was believed that the creature responsible for them had a misshapen foot, which would have affected its gait. The tracks had been made in snow in December 1969 at Bossburg in Washington State and were transposed into plaster casts. Not only did Krantz study these casts himself, but he also sought independent advice on the dermal ridges that were apparent on the casts.

He used biomechanical modeling in order to build up a likely image of what had made the tracks. These tests indicated that the footprints were most likely created by a creature that stood approximately 8 feet (2.44 m) in height and weighed about 800 pounds (363 kg), findings seemingly in line with previous estimates and reported sightings of Bigfoot.

Distinguishing Truth from Reality

Nevertheless, as so often occurs in such investigations, the situation was not clear-cut. Unfortunately, the person who had drawn the attention of the Bigfoot research community to these tracks set alarm bells ringing when it turned out that he was known as a fraudster. This was at a time before today's advanced scientific methods could be applied to such investigations. Basically, much depended on basic analysis of straightforward visual evidence, be it footprints, photographs, or film.

In fact, just two years earlier, the world had been rocked by what has since become known as the Patterson-Gimlin film. There have been so many sightings of Bigfoot that you would expect good photographic evidence to be available by now. Yet again, however, this is not the case. Possibly this is because most people encounter Bigfoot unexpectedly and fear prevents an immediate reaction, even when a camera is available. As mentioned, encounters are usually brief in any event, and for some reason, even with modern digital equipment, the failure to obtain visual evidence seems more common than would be expected. Nevertheless, this striking film of a female Bigfoot left most experts puzzled. It was taken by former rodeo rider and Bigfoot researcher Roger Patterson in 1967, in the pre-digital era.

In the company of Bob Gimlin, he was riding through Bluff Creek, California. Suddenly, alongside a stream, they saw a Bigfoot, which caused their horses to rear up in fright. Patterson set off on foot, with a ciné camera, in pursuit of the creature. Much of the film is blurred as he ran over the uneven ground, but at one point, when he slowed down, the result was startling, and modern technology has helped to stabilize the image more effectively. What appears to be a Bigfoot is seen to turn toward the camera, revealing its facial features for a brief period, before disappearing into the surrounding forest.

Apart from the film, the two men made casts of the tracks left in the sand by the creature. It is interesting that the impressions left by the men themselves are shallow by comparison. This evidence at least superficially corresponds with the observations of Dr. Krantz.

In the excitement of the moment, however, Patterson failed to record the speed at which he had taken the film. This could have clinched the issue beyond doubt. If it had been at 16 frames per second, then the creature shown on the film certainly had a significantly different gait from that of a human. Such a conclusion could not be drawn if the speed had been set at 24 frames per second.

In spite of this problem, the general conclusion of experts, including doctors with specialized knowledge of human movement, was that if the film is a fake, then it is extraordinarily successful. Special-effects creators said at the time that they would find it impossible to produce the detailed features of the creature captured on the film. Another specialist, in the field of ape suits, confirmed that in order to create the muscular movements evident in the film, a suit would need to cling tightly to the skin of the person within. It would not have been possible to use any form of padding to produce the effect.

Yet not all experts were convinced about the authenticity of Patterson's film and the casts of the footprints taken. The late Dr. Don Grieve (1931–2009) who was professor of biomechanics at the Royal Free Hospital School of Medicine in London (and later based at University College, London), examined the film very closely and concluded that the creature was no taller than 6.5 feet (1.95 m). According to Patterson, however, the footprints were nearly 15 inches (37.5 cm) long. Calculations suggested that the height of the Bigfoot should therefore have been over 8 feet (2.4 m). Moreover, the distance between footprints, said to be 3.5 feet (1.2 m), is too short for an animal of nearly 6.5 feet (1.95 m), let alone 8 feet (2.4 m). If Grieve was correct, then it appears that the film and the evidence of the footprints cannot both be genuine. Nevertheless, the Patterson-Gimlin film remains for many quite conclusive evidence supporting the existence of Bigfoot.

Later Doubts Emerge

But there is a further bizarre twist to the story, which surfaced in 2004, calling the film's authenticity into more serious doubt. It involved Philip Morris, a magician turned leading Hollywood costume-creator. Back in 1967, Morris had begun his business by making gorilla suits in the basement of his home in Charlotte, North Carolina. They had become popular because of a popular carnival trick at the time where a woman is transformed into a seemingly aggressive gorilla, which often led to some visitors running out the tent!

Morris described how a man named Roger Patterson got in touch with him to buy one of these suits. He recalled how, subsequently, Patterson contacted him to ask how he could make it look even more realistic, and he passed on some tips, including wearing football shoulder pads to suggest increased bulk, and ensuring the fur was brushed so that it covered the zipper. After that, so Morris claimed, he never heard from Patterson again.

He was sitting at home watching television in October 1967, however, when he saw the Patterson-Gimlin film. At this stage, though, Morris decided not to come forward to reveal the hoax, as he did not wish to undermine a fellow illusionist, who had quite clearly captured the public's attention. He therefore waited until long after Patterson's death in 1972, before telling his story.

News about it reached author Greg Long, who was working on a book about Bigfoot at the time. Having subsequently interviewed Morris on four separate occasions, he was convinced that the film had featured his suit, particularly as aspects of its design linked with information that Long had gleaned from a man named Bob Heironimus, who was supposedly wearing the suit when the film was made.

Yet, as ever in the case of Bigfoot, opinion is deeply divided. On one hand, if it was a specially created suit, then Morris would certainly have been one of the leading candidates to provide it. He worked at the top level in the film industry before AI effectively eliminated much of the need for costumes of this type. Among Morris's film credits were the white gorilla suit that features in the 1971 film *Diamonds Are Forever*—the seventh of the highly popular James Bond movie franchise.

But Bigfoot researchers dismiss Morris's claims, drawing on aspects of the film in their defense. They highlight the natural appearance of the lie of the fur, as well as the proportions of the body, which are in keeping with a creature of that size. Morris himself passed away on September 24, 2017, at eighty-three years of age, taking whatever else he knew about this strange event to the grave.

Soaring Popularity

In recent years, the Bigfoot/Sasquatch phenomenon has entered popular culture to an unparalleled extent. This has led to portrayals of these creatures in a wide range of films, as well as a number of significant investigative television series into the Bigfoot phenomenon, bringing the subject to international audiences. These began notably with *Finding Bigfoot* (2011), which ran for 101 episodes in total, with the latest incarnation being *Expedition Bigfoot*, which first hit the screens in 2019. This series in particular has sought to introduce the latest scientific technology into the hunt for this mysterious cryptid, and the outcomes, although still not definitive as yet, have nevertheless been gripping.

Bigfoot has also appeared in a wide range of advertising, in addition to being portrayed as toys and in both board and video games. It has been the inspiration behind many stories published in books and a variety of songs, in genres ranging from country to punk. Over the past fifty years or so, Bigfoot has transformed from a mysterious creature into a commercial phenomenon, irrespective of whether it exists or not!

Although most scientists believe that Bigfoot is a legend, the possibility that it may be alive has nevertheless led to the introduction of legislation banning hunting of such creatures, as any living Bigfoot would be in great danger from hunters looking to capitalize on its fame. But ironically, under the rules for naming species, there has to be an example, referred to as the "type specimen," available in a museum for study, in order for the species to be officially recognized by science. This would then allow it to be granted full protection under existing laws and treaties, just as in the case of other endangered species.

Lifestyle Investigations

Sasquatches are believed to live individually, in pairs, or as small family groups, rather than associating together in larger numbers. Clearly, if they do exist, they are scarce and may spend time on the move as well. They might undertake seasonal movements within their range in the Pacific Northwest, possibly to breeding grounds farther south.

Attempts by researchers to prove Bigfoot's existence have increasingly focused on examining and attempting to investigate the potential lifestyle of Sasquatches in the first instance. This approach offers an opportunity to confirm that they are real, alongside more tangible associated evidence such as hair samples that can be scientifically verified. This approach could undoubtedly confirm they are another member of the Hominidae family alongside great apes and ourselves, thereby discounting Bigfoot as being a shape-shifting entity from another dimension. Aspects of their natural history, such as their social structure and the various ways in which they can communicate, are now contributing to building up a picture of not only how such creatures might live but also how they can be discovered, using advances in technology, including the use of DNA.

It is well known that great apes such as gorillas and chimpanzees construct fresh nests for sleeping purposes. Unexplained nests of this type have also been found repeatedly in areas where Sasquatch reports are commonplace, sometimes even with two or three close to each other, suggesting their use by a family group. It is hard to explain these carefully crafted roughly circular, terrestrial structures, lined with fresh leaves, given that there is no known native North American species that would construct beds of this type.

Equally bizarre are wooden structures of significant height that apparently seem to serve as distinctive features in the landscape and are often encountered well off the beaten track. They commonly take the form of long branches or sapling trees that have been uprooted and driven back into the ground with considerable force—far more than would be generally assumed that a human could muster without the assistance of machinery. It has been suggested that these are territorial markers of some kind, constructed by Sasquatches to indicate their presence in an area to others. These structures vary in shape and complexity, but it is the upturned trees or broken branches, driven back into the ground that allow them to be recognized, sometimes positioned so they lean up against other trees in a clearing, if not in more open ground.

Sasquatches are generally thought to be crepuscular, meaning that they become active as daylight fades, and remain active for a period after dark. One particular aspect of Bigfoot reports that sets them apart from other primates and fits in with this lifestyle seemingly relates to the anatomy of their eyes.

Reports often refer to the green or reddish eye shine that stands out when a light is shone toward a Sasquatch. This is common in many animals that are more active after dark, such as cats, and it results from a reflective layer known as the *tapetum lucidum*, which lies behind the retina at the back of each eye. Its purpose is to reflect light that has passed through the eye, helping to improve the quality of the image when light levels are low.

As far as primates are concerned, however, this feature has not been recorded in the case of ourselves or any other living apes, although it is associated with the smaller strepsirrhine primates, such as the lemurs found in Madagascar and lorises from parts of Asia. No member of this group occurs in the Americas today, although their fossilized remains have been found there. While it is not beyond the bounds of possibility that this feature could have evolved in the case of Bigfoot, it would therefore mark such a species out as being quite distinctive from other living hominids.

The Significance of Sound

A different approach to investigating the Sasquatch mystery was begun by a journalist named Alan Berry. In 1972, he visited a remote, inaccessible part of northern California within the High Sierra Mountains, where various sightings of these creatures had been reported. Relying on a cassette tape recorder, Berry was able to capture what he maintained were the eerie calls of the creature on his machine. These have become known as the Sierra sound recordings. Berry's cassette tape was submitted for specialist examination, which formed a year-long project at the University of Wyoming. The conclusions were that the tape had not been tampered with to produce the sounds, and they were likely to have been made by creatures similar to humans but of a larger size. Most significantly, though, the view was that there were linguistic patterns evident within the recordings. The range and frequency were beyond that of humans as well, lessening the likelihood that the Sierra Sounds could have been faked. Two years later, Berry's colleague Ron Morehead returned to the same area and recorded a series of similar sounds.

Other researchers have suggested that Sasquatches can utter a series of calls of a howling nature that are capable of traveling over some distance.

Field investigators have used such sounds seemingly to set up a brief dialogue with these creatures, yet without drawing them into a close encounter. It is nevertheless very difficult to rely on calls as evidence for Bigfoot's existence, since various animals can make the very unusual sounds on occasion, that can be easily misinterpreted by the untrained ear. Others have pointed out that there also appears to be no characteristic consistency in the reported calls attributed to Bigfoot across its range, compared with the roar of a lion for example.

Sound has nevertheless played a significant ongoing role in terms of Bigfoot research, as there has been a widespread belief that these creatures may frequently communicate not necessarily by direct calls but by another method, known as "wood-knocking." The theory is that they might strike short, thick branches against trees, with the resulting sound traveling a surprising distance, particularly in the relatively quiet environment of the forest at night. Communicating in this way, rather than using direct vocalizations, would undoubtedly help to conceal the actual presence of Bigfoot in the area. The use of wood-knocking as a part of Sasquatch investigation work has garnered unexpected responses in terms of corresponding knocks being made in reply. As a result, it has become a routine method used by researchers out in the field. This method of communication may provide a way for Sasquatches to keep in touch without revealing their identity through vocalizations and may also serve as a method to mark territories over a wide area.

Some researchers have suggested that Sasquatches also use low-frequency sound, known as infrasound, for this purpose. This is the same means of long-distance communication that African elephants are known to use, which enables them to keep in touch over a distance of up to 6 miles (10 km). The sound waves travel through the ground, and the vibrations are detected through the elephants' feet, helping individuals to find each other. Nor are they alone in communicating in this way; whales display such behavior as well and are able to locate other members of their species over much longer distances because ultrasound waves travel much farther in the world's oceans.

Other animals, including rhinoceroses and giraffes, are known to use ultrasound for communication, but this ability has not been detected in any great ape, and we ourselves cannot hear the low-frequency notes that characterize this type of sound. Thus, this is another potential characteristic that would make Bigfoot unique among hominids.

New Technologies

An array of the latest high-tech equipment is now being employed in the search for definite evidence that would confirm the existence of Sasquatches. Drones with a wide range of abilities are now routinely used for this purpose. They can help to highlight movement on the ground, thereby serving to direct researchers from above, and are also able to capture photographic images. Aerial drones can even help to scan the ground and build up a map of the terrain under tree cover, highlighting possible "cold spots" that could indicate caves. Investigators believe that these may serve as retreats for Bigfoot on occasion.

Perhaps rather surprisingly, there are actually a number of difficulties when it comes to tracking a large animal in the type of terrain said to be inhabited by Sasquatches: not least is the fact that these wooded areas are often full of shadows, and given the dark appearance of these creatures generally, they would merge very effectively into the backdrop of the forest. This makes it difficult to detect them, with surrounding trees and bushes breaking up their outline. Furthermore, the much bigger stride length of a Sasquatch, based on accounts of its size and tracks, would mean that it could easily outpace a human, with its greater strength assisting it to climb steep banks and wade across rivers more easily.

Almost certainly, if they do exist, Sasquatches would follow game paths through the forest when possible. These would offer easier routes along which they could travel, being created by more numerous animals such as deer, which keep the vegetation down-trodden. These trails are evident as recognizable paths running through the surrounding forest. This in turn means that researchers can place trail cameras attached to trees at suitable heights along such routes with a view to capturing a clear image of a Sasquatch as it moves along the track. These battery-operated devices are able to record on memory cards over a considerable period of time, being triggered to start recording by movement in their vicinity, and they are also weather resistant.

Nevertheless, some researchers have reported finding devices of this type being ripped down and smashed on the ground on occasions. This suggests that a Sasquatch may be able to detect the presence of these trail cameras set to its height, even though they usually have a camouflaged outer case that may look like tree bark. It has been suggested that the non-ionizing electromagnetic fields (EMF) created by such cameras may be detected by Sasquatches. This output is claimed to trigger the creatures into ripping these devices off trees and other locations where they have been attached. Interestingly, such cameras are more likely to remain undisturbed when researchers place EMF-blocking jackets over them. This serves to conceal their presence more effectively, as they are no longer emitting radiation.

Since Bigfoot is believed to be predominantly active after dark, spotting it at this stage of the day is clearly more difficult than doing so when it is light. But once again, technology has made this more straightforward, thanks to infrared or thermal imaging cameras that detect heat signatures and can be either hand-held or fitted to drones. Nowadays, there is also the option of military-grade nighttime googles.

Physical evidence that might indicate the presence of a Sasquatch in an area can also be collected and subjected to the latest scientific analysis in laboratories. Hair samples in particular could provide irrefutable evidence of the existence of these mysterious creatures. It is assumed that their hairs, in common with those of other primates, will lack a central core, known as the medulla, running down the length of the hair. Examining hair samples under an ordinary microscopic will pick up this feature or highlight its absence, which gives a clue, albeit not a definite identification.

Hairs with their follicles attached, which mark the point of attachment within the body, provide an opportunity to obtain DNA as well, and thus unmask the individual's unique genetic code, helping to reveal its identity. A more recent and exciting refinement in this area is what is known as eDNA, which stands for environmental DNA. This could ultimately prove particularly invaluable in areas where Sasquatches are thought to have built nests of sticks. One of the difficulties when searching for a creature of this type is the sheer vastness and relative inaccessibility of the terrain where it may be present. Now, though, science has made it possible to look back in time and detect creatures that have passed through the area. This is because as an animal moves it sheds cells from its body that contain DNA, especially in locations where it is suspected of spending time sleeping, for example. It is even possible to collect and study eDNA in water, which is potentially significant because there are numerous accounts of Sasquatches being associated with stretches of water, wading out in search of fish.

A Scientific Search for Mysterious Hominids

As a result of the increasing reliance on technology when searching, therefore, the likelihood of a creature such as Bigfoot being able to remain out of sight is becoming correspondingly reduced. Some of the results obtained have already proved quite interesting, although not necessarily in the way that Bigfoot advocates would have hoped! A significant joint study, carried out in 2012 by scientists from the University of Oxford and the Museum of Zoology in Lausanne, Switzerland, asked for hair samples said to have originated from Sasquatches and other mysterious primates presently unrecognized by science.

In total, the team received fifty-seven hairs from both museums and private collections dating from as far back as fifty years. Out of this total, twenty were dismissed at the outset as being either too damaged to study, or because they were actually derived from plants rather than animals! When it comes to obtaining good DNA results, it is important that the specimen is collected with as little cross-contamination as possible, which is why these days researchers carry gloves and other equipment in the field specifically for this purpose.

However, many of the samples that were sent in for analysis were badly cross-contaminated with human DNA as the result of repeated handling by people through the years. They therefore needed to be effectively cleaned within the laboratory environment before testing could get underway. It was particularly important to avoid confusion in this instance, given any possible relationship between humans and Sasquatches.

From the sample of thirty-seven hairs that were subsequently examined, seven were found to lack sufficient DNA for testing purposes. The sources of the remaining hairs were then all identified successfully, however, yielding the

DNA of known species. The majority were derived from bears, although they actually covered a variety of other animals too, ranging from domestic species such as cattle and horses to more unexpected sources such as raccoons and even a porcupine!

The Broader Picture

Although the majority of reports of Bigfoot emanate from the Pacific Northwest, there are also significant numbers from Colorado and Texas and a cluster in states bordering the Great Lakes, while Florida remains a hot-spot for sightings as well. This raises the obvious question as to whether the same unknown species could be represented in all these areas.

One of the most frustrating aspects of the Bigfoot story, seized upon by those who do not believe in the existence of a large unidentified hominid in North America, is the absence of physical evidence. There are varied and quite regular reports of such creatures being seen crossing highways for example, notably from dusk onward, and yet there has never been an account of a creature being killed in a collision with a vehicle. Bearing in mind the almost incalculable number of journeys undertaken by vehicles through areas where Bigfoot reports have been made over the course of many decades, this does seem to be a significant argument against its existence.

Extending this line of skeptical thinking further, there has also obviously never been a case of the remains of a Bigfoot being discovered in the wider countryside either. This, however, may be easier to explain, being a reflection of what is believed to be the lifestyle of such creatures. First, no one believes that Sasquatches are common, even if they do exist, and furthermore, it has been suggested that they not only roam over vast, inaccessible areas but they may also be migratory, at least in some areas. The belief is that, as apes, Sasquatches would have a lifespan similar to our own and live individually, in pairs, or in small family groups.

This all adds up to the fact that the chances of finding their remains in the vast wilderness of the Pacific Northwest would be quite small. Moreover, it has been suggested (albeit without evidence) that family groups may bury their dead or place them in caves, which would serve to explain the lack of skeletal remains found in the open.

If the Sasquatch is not a real creature, however, how does one explain the many thousands of supposed sightings that have been made? There are some who regard Sasquatches as shapeshifters, able to disappear into their environment but then physical evidence, such as hair or DNA would be lacking, emphasizing the fact that they would not be actual animals, as we define them.

Coming from the busy cities in which many of us live today, it is obvious that venturing out into areas of wilderness takes us into a radically different environment. Our senses are heightened in this type of setting, magnifying sounds that we detect, ironically because these surroundings are much quieter than those we generally experience in our daily lives. The breaking of branches, for example, sounds louder. Fleeting images that we detect out of the corners of our eyes assume more of a significance, particularly in an environment where animals such as bears that can kill us are to be found.

The farther that you venture away from civilization into the wilderness, the more isolated you are likely to feel. It is quite common to start thinking you are being watched or even followed in such surroundings, walking along long-forgotten logging routes and stumbling across abandoned cabins. With the added suggestion that there are large, mysterious hominids in these areas, it is not surprising that you can end up convincing yourself that you did indeed have a fleeting encounter of some type with a Sasquatch.

As has been mentioned repeatedly, Sasquatch reports have attracted a wide range of chancers and outright fraudsters over the years. The appeal for such people is even greater today, given the instant worldwide profile that would arise from a convincing close encounter and the fortune that could then be generated, especially via social media.

Yet even if you dismiss the vast majority of Sasquatch sightings as misidentifications and others as deliberate deception, this still leaves a significant number that are difficult to explain away successfully. It is also worth emphasizing that native North American tribes tell stories of such creatures in their folklore, dating back many centuries. Are these simply figments of the imagination, or do they have a factual basis? And, if they are imagined, where has the inspiration for such stories originated? It is well documented that there have never been primates of any kind, let alone apes, native to North America during the period of human existence.

Possible Identities

A number of suggestions have been put forward to explain the Sasquatch's possible identity. There is what has sometimes been described as the "relic hominid theory," as espoused by Dr. Grover Krantz. He believed that they could represent the descendants of a population of giant apes known to science as *Gigantopithecus blacki*, which originated in Asia. Krantz believed that some individuals crossed into North America when the continents were joined together by the Bering Land Bridge. This is the same route by which it is believed that humans first entered North America. It might help to explain why Bigfoot sightings are most common today on the northwestern side of North America, as well as serving to account for reports of similar creatures in Alaska. The land bridge existed until the end of the last Ice Age, when rising sea levels finally swamped the link about eleven thousand years ago, creating what is known today as the Bering Strait.

The difficulty with this theory, however, is that *Gigantopithecus* is known to have lived in what is now southern China for a period beginning approximately two million years ago, before becoming extinct there around two hundred thousand years ago, based on our current knowledge. The Bering Land Bridge dates back seventy thousand years, but this is after the time that *Gigantopithecus* is thought to have become extinct, although it is fair to point out that we only have limited knowledge about these creatures, and they could well have been alive much later and potentially made this continental crossing.

Gigantopithecus was originally identified from two molar teeth, spotted in a traditional medicine outlet in China in 1935. Although since then its remains have been positively identified from at least sixteen sites, and the range of these apes has been extended more widely through southeast Asia, only a few jaw bones and a relatively large number of teeth have been discovered but no other parts of their skeleton. This therefore makes it very difficult to build up a detailed, accurate impression of what *Gigantopithecus* would have looked like in life, particularly in terms of its size. But what is clear is that its molar teeth, located at the back of the mouth, are the biggest on record for an ape. It is believed to have fed on a varied diet of forest plants and fruits. The very thick enamel coating on the teeth, measuring up to 0.25 inch (6 mm), gave good protection for a lifetime's wear. Bigfoot in contrast is believed to be omnivorous in its feeding habits, eating a variety of plants, fruits, and berries according to the season, while also actively hunting prey, such as white-tailed deer (*Odocoileus virginianus*). The skeletal remains of the deer have sometimes been documented in unusual locations, such as high up in trees. Researchers suggest that these carcasses may have been placed here by Sasquatches.

It is now clear that *Gigantopithecus* was most closely related to today's orangutan species, based on a study of the amino acid compositions of the proteins present in both the dentine and outer enamel covering of their teeth. As it is not possible to correlate body and tooth sizes accurately, it may well be that *Gigantopithecus* was not as large as has been speculated based on its dental remains. Furthermore, orangutans are essentially arboreal by nature, whereas accounts of Sasquatches reveal a strong link to a terrestrial lifestyle. It therefore seems increasingly unlikely that this relic hominid theory provides an explanation for today's Sasquatch sightings.

However, this does not entirely rule out the possibility of some sightings being explained by modern-day apes. Across the United States, apes have misguidedly been kept as pets. Some of these have either escaped or have been deliberately released into the wild. Although it may not be a case where a breeding population has become established, occasional sightings from a distance could be suggestive of a Sasquatch, particularly in an area where the latter are reputed to occur. This modern primate theory could represent a particularly likely explanation in terms of explaining sightings of Florida's Skunk Ape. The climate in this part of the country is much more conducive to allowing primates such as orangutans or chimpanzees to thrive.

There could be other explanations too, in terms of sightings. Some people choose to live a solitary existence well off the beaten track, away from other people. Unfortunately, on a few occasions, those living in this way, especially when glimpsed briefly in poor light, have been mistaken for Sasquatches and even shot. This situation was most common after the Vietnam War, which ended in 1975. An unknown number of American veterans, often suffering from posttraumatic stress disorder (PTSD), chose to disappear "off the grid" and lived in the wilds of Washington State. Even today, occasional hermits may still be encountered unexpectedly in this area where Sasquatch sightings are made.

Undoubtedly, though, one of the most common and credible explanations for Sasquatch sightings is confusion with American black bears (*Ursus americanus*), which roam in the same areas where such reports are commonly made. The relatively solitary lifestyle of these bears also links with observations of Sasquatches, and they are typically brownish in color, as well as being covered in hair.

A highly significant behavior of bears in this context is the fact that they may often stand up on their hind legs, which gives them a height approximating to that of a Sasquatch when seen from a distance. In addition, they can also move on their hind legs, creating bipedal tracks. There is also the possibility that their hind feet could fit into the tracks created by their front feet when moving on the ground, creating a similar impression.

Although bears will attack people, particularly in the case of a female with her cubs, they tend to avoid contact, and when they detect a human presence, they will drop down onto all four legs and disappear into the forest. In addition, bears tend to be crepuscular by nature, becoming more active as darkness descends, so they are most likely to disappear into the shadows.

However, there is one aspect of ursine biology that suggests that bear sightings can only account for a percentage of Sasquatch sightings. This is because of the fact that American black bears generally hibernate through much of their range, especially in northern areas. Only in southernmost parts, down in Mexico for example, does the population not display this behavior consistently. This therefore suggests that bears cannot be responsible for Sasquatch reports made during the winter period, when they are asleep in their dens.

While the distribution of the black bear overlaps closely with that of the Sasquatch, the brown bear (*Ursus arctos*) is confined to the far north, where it has an almost circumpolar range. It too lives mainly in forested areas and is omnivorous in its feeding habits. This species can potentially account for at least some sightings of Sasquatches especially in the vicinity of Alaska, which has proved to be an active area for Bigfoot encounters over the past century. Interestingly, reports of Sasquatch-type creatures, known locally in this area of North America as *nantiinaq*, suggest that they are more aggressive than those occurring elsewhere, mirroring the difference in biology between these two species of bear. There was the famous case of the southern Alaskan town of Portlock, lying on the Kenai Peninsula, which was established as a salmon cannery but ended up being abandoned in the mid-twentieth century after a number of people went missing and sightings of tall dark, Bigfoot-like figures were made in the surrounding countryside.

The link between Sasquatch reports and bears was originally investigated in 2009, by a team led by Professor Michael Hickerson in the Pacific Northwest. Then in 2024, it was repeated by researcher Floe Floxon, across all of the United States and Canada, comparing the density of bears with the number of Sasquatch sightings. She discovered that where bears were most numerous, so too were sightings of Sasquatches.

The only place that this did not at first glance correspond in terms of a correlation was in the state of Florida. But here, the situation is rather different, not least because there are fewer forests. In addition, though, the human population of the Sunshine State is significantly higher, consisting of some twenty-two million people, compared with just eight million living in Washington State, where the recorded number of Sasquatch sightings are similar. These factors suggest that there are likely to be more sightings in Florida partly because there are more people, while additionally, the majority of black bears (except females with cubs) will remain active throughout the year.

A Global Perspective

It is worth remembering that although today Sasquatch may be the best-known mystery hominid, it is certainly not alone, according to reports from around the world. This too could actually be significant in unravelling the mystery. In fact, up until the latter half of the twentieth century, the yeti or "abominable snowman" recorded from the Himalayan region in Asia had arguably attracted more attention, thanks to stories brought back by Western mountaineers and others who were venturing into this remote region with increasing frequency.

The story of the yeti mirrors that of Sasquatch, in a number of significant ways. First, there is local folklore, reinforced in this case by ancient relics preserved in monasteries. Second, there are supposed sightings of the creature itself, or indications of its presence in the area, such as footprints.

Many leading mountaineers, including Sir Edmund Hillary and sherpa Tenzing Norgay who were the first to climb Mount Everest in 1953, recorded seeing inexplicable large footprints on the mountain and even figures in the distance. Seven years later, Hillary set out on a new expedition specifically to investigate reports of the yeti. He borrowed a scalp said to come from the remains of a yeti housed in a monastery, bringing it back to London where it could be examined. Although it was at a time before DNA investigations were possible, comparative analysis suggested that this artifact was actually derived not from a primate but from a local animal known as a serow (*Capricornis sumatraensis thar*) which resembles a goat in appearance.

More recent investigations have all drawn a blank. Hair samples from the Garo Hills in northeastern India were revealed to have come from a Himalayan gorai (*Naemorhedus goral*), a species of bovid native to the Himalayas. Interestingly, it appears that bears actually account for most sightings of yetis, based on DNA findings—most notably Himalayan brown bears (*Ursus arctos isabellinus*), as revealed by those samples submitted for examination by scientists at the Universities of Oxford and Lausanne (see page 155). Follow-up research confirmed that supposed yeti hairs also came from the Tibetan blue bear (*Ursus arctos pruinosus*) (which is another distinctive form of the brown bear), as well as the Asiatic black bear (*Ursus thibetanus*).

Yet one part of the world where bears are most unlikely to explain sightings of large, unknown hominids is in Australia. There are no records of bears on this continent. Nevertheless, there have been persistent reports of giant hominids extending back into the ancient lore of the native Aboriginal people living here. Popularly known as the Yowie, such creatures are believed to inhabit the Blue Mountains, in the southeastern parts of the country which has the highest incidence of sightings. Other areas where encounters have been reported include the Springbrook area of southeastern Queensland and around the Acacia Hills in Northern Territory.

The description of "Yowie" is believed to derive from the language of the Kámilarói people, as documented in Rev. William Ridley's book entitled *Kámilarói and Other Australian Languages*, which was published in 1875. The word, written phonetically as *Yō-wī*, describes a spirit that reputedly roams the earth at night.

The earliest recorded report of a Yowie was in a magazine published in February 1842. Described as being about the same height as a man, with very long arms and white hair on the head, it was regarded as an ape-like creature. A subsequent account from 1882 suggested that the color of the hair on its chest differed from the black hair covering the rest of its body.

Residents in the vicinity of the Blue Mountains have continued to report Yowie sightings to the present day, and these more recent encounters tend to suggest that the creature itself is taller than initially suggested. One of the leading proponents of the Yowie's existence was a dedicated investigator named Rex Gilroy. By the time of his death in 2023, he had amassed an archive comprised of more than five thousand recorded accounts and sightings.

Long arms in primates are typically a sign of an arboreal lifestyle, aiding the creature in swinging through its forest home, as typified by orangutans (*Pongo* species). The Yowie's feet are also said to be much bigger than those of a person, but there is considerable variability in appearance when it comes to reported Yowie tracks. Once again, though, there is no convincing irrefutable physical evidence to suggest the Yowie is a physical being, nearly two hundred years after it first became documented by European settlers.

Another cryptid hominid reportedly lives in the mountains of central Asia, occurring here in the Caucasus and neighboring regions, ranging to the Altai Mountains in western Mongolia. Variously known as the alma, almas, or almasty, the name of these mysterious creatures features within the Mongolian landscape, which in turn suggests a long-standing belief in their existence. As an example, there is the *Almasyn Dobo*, translating as the "Hills of the Almases," which lie in the southwest of Mongolia.

One of the earliest surviving accounts of the alma comes from the explorer and spy Nikolay Przhevalsky (1839–1888), who traveled widely through the region, ostensibly as a naturalist. He certainly made some remarkable zoological discoveries, including the only surviving species of wild equid, known as Przewalski's horse (*Equus przewalskii*), as well as the rodent known as the Mongolian gerbil (*Meriones unguiculatus*), which has subsequently become a popular pet worldwide, although confirmatory proof of the almas's existence eluded him.

Nevertheless, Przhevalsky recorded that it was said to possess the flattened face of a person, with its feet equipped with powerful claws and its body covered in dense black fur. Reputed to be very powerful, this "man-beast" or *kung-guressu* was often bipedal, walking upright on its hind legs. It inspired fear even among hunters as well as people living in the area, causing them to move away on occasions.

Interestingly, Przhevalsky's account of the alma does provide several potential clues as to the identity of the creature, which have tended to be confirmed by much more recent scientific testing carried out by teams from the universities of Oxford and Lausanne (see page 155) as part of a general survey of hair samples believed to come from mysterious hominids worldwide. Although the results were surprisingly varied, the evidence suggested that the only animal found in the study capable of walking on two legs would be the brown bear (*Ursus arctos*). In spite of its name, it is known that the fur color of the brown bear can vary, being very dark brown and even blackish on occasions, in the case of individuals found in parts of Europe and Asia. Furthermore, certainly when seen in the shadows of a forest, these bears do appear to be much darker in appearance than may otherwise be the case.

However, not everyone is convinced by this explanation. They highlight what are believed to be the earliest documented reports of these mysterious hominids, which date back to the early 1400s. A German traveler named Johann (Hans) Schiltberger (1380–c. 1440), ended up being taken prisoner by Turkish forces and subsequently wrote about his experiences in this region, which was largely unknown at that stage. The surrounding mountains, then regarded as being on the very edge of the world, were said to be home to a population of wild people, who walked in a bipedal way but were totally covered in hair. Only the palms of their hands and soles of their feet were hairless, according to Schiltberger's account.

Reports have continued down the centuries. In 2008, an expedition to the region where almas are believed to occur, involving members of the Centre for Fortean Zoology, discovered a number of eye-witnesses who claimed to have had recent encounters with these creatures. The team returned with a population estimate of between one hundred and three hundred almas surviving in the region, but unfortunately, potential physical evidence in the form of hairs brought back with them did not reveal the alma's existence based on subsequent DNA analysis.

The question remains, if almas do exist, what are they? More recently, it has been suggested that almas may represent an isolated and remote population of neanderthals which still inhabits this part of Asia. Neanderthals are closely related to modern humans, and it has emerged from genetic studies of modern humans that they interbred with our ancestors. Known to science as *Homo neanderthalensis*, their range extended from Western Europe, including the Iberian peninsula and what is now southern England eastwards as far as the Altai Mountains.

There is clear evidence that neanderthals were distinctly smaller than modern-day humans, with the average height of men being just 5 feet 5 inches (165 cm), while women were approximately 5 inches (12.5 cm) shorter. In terms of their overall physique, based on their skeletal remains, neanderthals were stockier, with distinctly larger heads and shorter, muscular limbs than ourselves.

Unfortunately, there are still significant gaps in our understanding of the human family tree. It is currently believed that modern humans (*Homo sapiens*) emerged about two hundred thousand to three hundred thousand years ago, in eastern Africa, before initially starting to move northward into Europe. Here they met neanderthals and various other types of archaic humans, which had all subsequently died out by forty thousand years ago, although, as mentioned, certainly in the case of neanderthals, a number of their genes still live on within some of us.

In 2003, a remarkable discovery was made in a cave on the Indonesian island of Flores, by a joint team of Australian-Indonesian archaeologists. They were searching for evidence to show the movement of people from Asia to Australia. Instead, they stumbled upon the remains of a totally undocumented species of human. Further excavations have revealed the remains of more than fifteen partial skeletons in this locality, all characterized by their small size. Now known to science as *Homo floresiensis*, they attained an adult height of just 3 feet 7 inches (1.1 m), and although initially, it was thought that this population may have survived up to as recently as twelve thousand years ago, subsequent analysis has revealed that these hominids actually died out earlier, about fifty thousand years ago.

This find is significant not only because of the small size of these early humans but also because it confirms that there could be other ancestral human forms still to be discovered. Unfortunately, we have exceedingly little insight into the relationships between the different *Homo* species and even how well they could communicate with each other when they came into contact. But it is more than possible, particularly in areas short of natural resources and food, that conflict would have arisen at times. There would probably have been an instinctive, deep-seated fear and suspicion between the different groups as a result throughout their associated histories.

A New Explanation?

Just as some neanderthal genes can still survive in our DNA today, is it possible that there could be a general link back to our distant ancestral past, explaining recorded sightings of not just the Sasquatch but all the other mystery hominids reputed to be found around the world? This seems to be potentially more likely now, especially as it emerges that there was a wider range of hominids that used to exist than previously thought.

It is exceedingly difficult, drawing on the numerous reported sightings over centuries from not just North America, where Bigfoot and other associated variants are reported to roam but also parts of Asia down into Australia, to understand how these mysterious hominids could remain hidden for so long. A battery of high-tech methods has been used over recent years in the search, and yet still nothing irrefutable in terms of scientific evidence has been unearthed to confirm the existence of Bigfoot or similar creatures elsewhere.

So could there be another possible reason for all the different reports of encounters from various parts of the world? This is indeed possible, reflecting a theory about how our brains collect and process information, which was put forward by the Swiss psychologist Carl G. Jung (1875–1961). We still know relatively little about the precise functioning of various areas of our brains. Jung proposed that each of us have a part of our brain given over to what he described as "collective unconsciousness." He believed that this part of our memory arose not from individual learning but was inherited from one generation to the next.

Deep subconscious images, which he termed "archetypes," would normally remain buried here. But it was possible, in Jung's view, for them to come to surface and enter the conscious mind, particularly if the person concerned was tired or under stress. These factors might therefore be sufficient to conjuror up frightening images and could generate a fleeting encounter with a long-extinct hominid relative from our distant past arising out of our deep ancestral consciousness.

It is easy to appreciate how, when out in unfamiliar terrain where there are dangerous animals such as bears and large wild cats, people can start to feel instinctively nervous, with their sensory systems becoming highly charged. Coupled with stories of a mysterious hominid such as Sasquatch seen in the same area and the changing effects of light, creating shadows in the landscape that might themselves appear to move around, is it surprising that the human imagination may go into overdrive? This sensation is probably more intense today than in the past, because of the divide between our essentially safe, urban lifestyles and these much more remote regions where predators are still present, and creatures such as the Sasquatch and the Yowie are said to roam. If you get the opportunity to visit such areas, we challenge you not to feel affected by the experience!

Ten Things You May Not Know About Sasquatches and Yetis

1 Following the death of the hoaxer Ray Wallace (see pages 147–8), the singer/songwriter Danny Freyer released what has become the unofficial anthem of Sasquatch believers, titled "The Bigfoot Song: I Still Believe in Bigfoot," in 2005.

2   The popular hit Bigfoot movie *Harry and the Hendersons*, which
    was released in 1987 and has grossed over $50 million worldwide,
    portraying Bigfoot not as a monster but as an intelligent and
    misunderstood being.

3   Bigfoot is commonly the subject of humorous internet memes, which
    often draw on false sightings or reflect its elusive nature.

4   A vast array of products featuring Bigfoot are now available, ranging
    from T-shirts and mugs to bobbleheads and bumper stickers,
    often featuring slogans like "Bigfoot Is Real" or "Gone Squatchin,"
    confirming its status as a modern icon.

5   A variety of festivals with a Bigfoot theme are held regularly, including
    Sasquatch Days in Harrison Hot Springs, Canada, and the Bigfoot
    Daze in Willow Creek, California. These celebrate the legend with
    parades, talks, and merchandise.

6   There are even theatrical productions featuring Bigfoot, notably
    Sasquatched! The Musical, which was the work of Phil Darg and
    premiered to a favorable critical reception in 2012.

7   Bigfoot has become a popular mascot, especially in the field of sports
    and notably at the 2010 Winter Olympics held in Vancouver, British
    Columbia, Canada, which introduced a young Sasquatch mascot called
    Quatchi to an international audience.

8   In 1959, the US Embassy in Nepal insisted that those searching for
    the yeti obtain permits in advance and report their findings to the
    Nepalese government.

9   In 2013, plans were announced for a yeti-themed resort in Siberia's
    Sheregesh ski area, which included a museum and hotel. There was
    also a significant reward on offer for anyone who could capture a Yeti,
    which remains unclaimed.

10 A supposed ancient finger of a yeti was taken without permission from
    Nepal's Pangboche Temple for testing abroad. It was smuggled out in
    the late 1950s allegedly with the help of the famous Hollywood actor
    James Stewart and his wife, Gloria, who supposedly hid the digit in
    among her lingerie. Subsequent testing revealed it had actually come
    from a human hand!

8

THE THUNDERBIRD
AND SIMILAR TALES

A carved image of a thunderbird.
Photo courtesy SvetlanaSF/www
.shutterstock.com

Tales about gigantic flying birds have been told for over four thousand years
by the tribes living on the Pacific Northwest coast of North America as well
as in the Northeast and Midwest, particularly among the Algonquian peoples.
Such stories about thunderbirds have nevertheless spread much further afield
across the continent, extending for example to the Iroquois whose homeland

on the opposite side of the continent extends from around the Great Lakes down to the American southwest and across the Great Plains.

Storms in this area can be quite ferocious, and at a stage when there was no understanding surrounding the causes of weather, the widespread belief arose that a giant bird was involved in controlling aspects of the weather above ground. The thunderbird generated the sounds of thunderclaps as it flapped its giant wings, and when it blinked, it was believed to cause lightning, reflecting the immense power that it was believed to possess.

Artistic Representations

Artifacts of thunderbirds dating back thousands of years have been unearthed on various ancient sites in North America. There is also a very distinctive portrayal of a thunderbird carved in sandstone, alongside various other animals, discovered near the Lemonweir River at Twin Bluffs in Juneau County, Wisconsin. These stone carvings or petroglyphs have been impossible to date, but it is clear that they were made at some stage in prehistory.

In recent times, representations of thunderbirds have traditionally featured in the totem poles of the Pacific Northwest. Carved from the relatively durable, local red cedar trees (*Thuja plicata*), these posts have been created in the region over the course of centuries, dating back to at least the 1600s and probably earlier.

In the early days, however, before iron was introduced to the region and incorporated into tools, carving was incredibly laborious and time-consuming. As a result, the early totem poles (which have now rotted away) are known to have been shorter and less complex than those created from the 1800s onward, when the advent of metal axes helped to facilitate the construction process. Yet this period was relatively short-lived, as a clampdown on local cultural practices saw carving of these poles essentially coming to an end by the start of the twentieth century.

Once carving ceased, those totem poles that were still in existence were simply abandoned and left to decay. Interest in this important cultural heritage resurfaced again, however, and in 1938, the United States Forest Service managed to salvage and restore about two hundred totem poles, representing approximately a third of those that had been standing at the turn of the century. Thunderbirds were usually incorporated right at the pinnacle of the pole, typically displaying the bright colors and sharp hooked bill considered to be their characteristic features.

The Algonquian regard the thunderbird as a god, locked in deadly combat with the ruler of the underworld, which is considered to be either an underwater panther or alternatively, a great horned serpent known as Misiginebig. The thunderous claps echo from its wings, while bolts of lightning spark off its bill, being directed down and striking the ground. The way that thunderbirds are portrayed in tribal imagery varies, often being shown in an X-shape, as in the Algonquian tradition, with the head portrayed in profile, although there are distinctive local tribal variances.

Reputed Lifestyle

Thunderbirds were believed to have lived above the highest mountains, usually flying in among the clouds there, but bad weather would force them down to lower levels where they could be seen by people. They are said to be far more powerful than other birds, sometimes being accompanied by eagles, which would appear to be small alongside them. According to some accounts, thunderbirds might also migrate with other birds, heading south at the start of winter and then returning to more northerly latitudes in spring. They reputedly lay rock-like eggs, which were known as thunderstones.

In spite of their strength and power, thunderbirds do not seek to attack people, and they might even help them, particularly during periods of famine or drought, although if they became angry, they could prove to be fearsome creatures. Some tribes credit them with the power of shape-shifting, with the Shawnee people of the Northeastern Woodlands believing them to manifest as boys, who were distinguishable by the fact that they spoke backwards.

It is therefore clear that there are aspects of mythology as well as real-life attributes that have become attached to thunderbirds, not least the fact that they are considered deities by various Native American people.

Close Encounters

But could the mythology surrounding the thunderbird be rooted in truth as we have seen in other cases? There are aspects of its natural history that suggest a living creature could explain the mystery and that it is not simply just a concoction of legend and fantasy. Remarkably, there are accounts of giant flying creatures from North America where thunderbirds were traditionally said to range, and such reports continue to be made right through until the present day.

One of the most remarkable events of this type took place the evening of July 25, 1977, when three boys were playing together outside in the town of Lawndale, Illinois. Two huge birds swooped down on them. One of the boys, Marlon Lowe, who weighed 65 pounds (30 kg) at the time, was seized and dragged about 2 feet (0.6 m) into the air, before he managed to free himself, by struggling and punching at the bird repeatedly.

His screams brought four adults running to the scene, all of whom witnessed the birds' presence and saw them fly off north, heading for a group of large trees growing along nearby Kickapoo Creek, after which they disappeared from view. Their descriptions of the birds' appearance were uniform, stating that the pair were both black in color, aside from a white ring of feathering encircling their long necks. There was less agreement in terms of their size, which is perhaps to be expected, because it is not easy to estimate the wingspans of birds in flight, particularly when they are airborne and some distance away.

The adult eyewitness who got closest to the birds during the encounter was Mrs. Ruth Lowe, the boy's mother. She thought their wingspans were probably between 8 and 10 feet (2.4–3 m) from tip to tip and estimated the length of their bodies as being approximately 4 feet (1.2 m) overall. She noted their large bills, which curved in a downward direction, like that of a bird of prey.

Later that day, Ruth Lowe contacted the authorities to report what had happened because she was worried about other children in the area. Unfortunately, her claims were met with widespread cynicism and disbelief, to the extent that she and the others involved were subjected to considerable personal abuse once the encounter was reported in the press, leading some of those present on that day to alter their statements.

Further Sightings

Yet this was not to be the end of the matter. While Ruth Lowe was seeking to identify the birds in question, sightings of strange birds started to be reported from elsewhere in the state. Some were identified more easily than others, such as the bird observed by Norma and Kenneth Knollenberg, who lived in New Holland, to the west of Lawndale. They spotted and photographed a large bird roosting on top of a barn at their farm, which transpired to be a peafowl— believed to be one of a group which, it subsequently emerged, was known to be living nearby.

It was clearly not similar in appearance to those encountered at Lawndale, nor indeed were a number of other large birds reported by members of the public at this stage, which were said to resemble cranes (which they may have been), or alternatively, some might easily have been herons. It is difficult, even for expert ornithologists, to assess the size of birds accurately when they are in flight as there is no obvious landmark to use by way of comparison in the sky, as when they are perching on a tree branch, for example.

But there were a series of other encounters that seemed very similar. Four days after the original, much publicized event, a mailman named James Majors was out doing an early morning round, driving in nearby Tazewell County when he spotted two huge birds flying overhead. As Majors paused to watch, one of the pair swooped down over a cornfield and seized a young pig in its talons, which he estimated must have weighed somewhere between 40 and 60 pounds (18–27 kg). Flapping its wings noisily, the bird then flew across the road, being as close as 30 feet (9 m) to his van, before flying off in a northerly direction with its partner.

Unfortunately, as these events occurred at about 5:50 a.m., there was no-one else around, but Majors was able to provide a good description. He estimated that its wingspan was approximately 8 feet (2.4 m) overall, and its powerful legs with its claws may have measured as much as 3.5 feet (1 m). Its strong bill was around 8 inches (20 cm) in length.

Reports of sightings of gigantic birds continued through in the region over the weekend, and some physical evidence was collected at this stage. A group of three friends spotted a solitary huge individual with a wingspan they estimated to be at least 6 feet (1.8 m), perched on a telegraph pole near Gillum, in south-central McLean County. It dropped something onto the ground, and the police subsequently found a dead rat that measured 1 foot (30 cm) in length on the ground under the pole, but by then the bird had flown.

Further Encounters

An even more engrossing tale with supporting evidence came from "Texas John" Huffer, an outdoorsman who was fishing on Lake Shelbyville along with his son later on that Saturday morning. It is worth noting that this is a large area of wilderness, extending over an area of approximately 11,000 acres (4,495 ha), located just 60 miles (97 km) from where the original sighting was made at Lawndale. The noise of the boat disturbed two birds that were in a tree, one of which was much bigger than its companion. This larger black individual, with an estimated wingspan of 12 feet (3.6 m), flew along from tree to tree, allowing Huffer, who had previously served as a combat photographer with the Marines, to film it. He described its call as being primeval.

In addition, when he went ashore at the point where they had first spotted the bird, Huffer noted droppings that were said to be the size of baseballs under the tree there. Unfortunately, it was not possible to carry out DNA analysis at that time, which might have played a key role in determining not just the origins of the dung but also potentially the identity of the large bird.

The evidence that Huffer did collect, however, in the form of his film, was soon dismissed as being just a turkey vulture (*Cathartes aura*). He challenged this view, highlighting the fact that the bird shown did not have a red ring around its neck, as does a turkey vulture, which, in any case, Huffer was very familiar with, and would have had no difficulty in identifying.

A further sighting followed at approximately 2 p.m. on the same day, in DeWitt County, which was again 60 miles (97 km) from the encounter recorded by the Huffers. The bird circled at this location but did not land and ultimately flew off and disappeared. Further reports followed on Sunday, July 31, but these turned out to be sightings of great blue herons (*Ardea herodias*).

The subject of gigantic bird encounters in Illinois then dropped off the news agenda until August 11. On that day, John and Wanda Chappell, who had a farm close to the village of Odin, south of Lake Shelbyville, spotted a massive bird through their closed glass doors while they were drinking coffee indoors. It was flying around close to their pond, came within 400 feet (122 m) of them, and apparently struggled to find a branch big enough to support its weight as it attempted to perch. John estimated its wingspan as between 10 and 12 feet (3.0–3.7 m) whereas Wanda considered it was more likely to be 14 feet (4.3 m), when comparing it with their boat which was present on the pond at that stage.

She dismissed the suggestion that it could have been a turkey vulture (or "buzzard" as these birds are often described locally), because again, she was used to seeing them in the area. As in the case of a vulture, she described it as having a featherless head, with a long crooked neck, charcoal or gray feathers on its body, and long legs.

The color of the plumage rules out the possibility of other large birds such as the wood stork (*Mycteria americana*), with its prominent white feathering. In any case, these wood storks have a very limited distribution, being confined mainly to coastal areas in the south. The same argument regarding plumage coloration applies in the case of the endangered whooping crane (*Grus americana*). The sandhill crane (*Antigone canadensis*) has a much wider distribution in North America, and does have gray plumage as well as very long legs, but equally, these cranes have very prominent red areas on their heads, which again rules them out.

The Final Total

After remaining in the tree in view of the Chappells for between five and ten minutes, the bird then took off, flying in a southwesterly direction toward the town of Centralia, bringing this remarkable series of sightings to a close. Although a number of reports were clearly cases of mistaken identity, there were at least nine encounters within a triangular-shaped area covering some 330 square miles (855 sq km) which could not be explained. Almost certainly, this figure was even higher over the course of the week, but because of the highly negative and indeed, even hostile reactions that sightings engendered among some people, both within the local community and media, there were others who failed to come forward.

The Search for an Explanation

There is no evidence to suggest that the bird was actually an escapee from a wildlife collection, although considerable media attention was given to a marabou stork (*Leptoptilos crumenifer*) that flew from its enclosure at the Brookfield Zoo. This, however, occurred on July 30, after the sightings began, and the bird was tracked flying north, crossing into the state of Wisconsin where it is known to have met a sad end.

Although successfully tranquilized, its fall from 70 feet (21 m) up in a tree to the ground proved to be fatal. Ultimately however, the expert view prevailed, with the unexplained sightings being regarded as turkey vultures, in spite of the fact that a number of witnesses such as the Huffers were exceedingly familiar with this particular bird of prey and were resolute that it was not what they saw, or indeed filmed, in this particular case.

Clues from the Past?

Perhaps strangely, no reference was made to Illinois's past ornithological history, on the part of the experts who were brought in to provide a rational explanation for this spate of mysterious sightings. If there had been, the outcome would probably have been a little less certain.

There had in fact been a previous series of reported sightings of gigantic birds in the state, not in such a localized area as happened in 1977, but extending more widely around the region of St. Louis and across the adjacent part of the border into Missouri. These lasted from January to the start of May 1948. Witnesses, including an army colonel, described the creature as being grayish in color and about the size of a Piper Club airplane. Indeed, it was said that it could be mistaken on this basis for a small airplane until it flapped its wings. One witness even described it as resembling a condor.

It is surprising that this thought did not feature as a possible explanation for the 1977 sightings. Condors are the largest flying land birds, not just in the Americas but throughout the entire Western Hemisphere. There are two species alive today, with the Andean condor (*Vultur gryphus*) confined to this mountain range in South America. Its wingspan can reach up to 10.5 feet (3.2 m) overall, with larger males attaining a weight of 33 pounds (15 kg).

While the likelihood of Andean condors reaching North America is exceedingly unlikely, it is quite within the bounds of possibility that the slightly smaller California condor (*Gymnogyps californianus*) might have been encountered in Illinois and elsewhere on the continent. The fact is that the status of this species has changed significantly over the course of the past century. Its numbers had declined to the stage that it was at the point of extinction by the time of the 1977 sightings.

An Overlooked Possibility

As a result, very few people would have seen or even been aware of these birds at that stage. Yet with a maximum wingspan of almost 10 feet (3 m), it is nevertheless the biggest bird to be found on the North American continent. Other features of the California condor include its long legs and, significantly, its bare neck has an area of white feathering, while the rest of its plumage is blackish, corresponding to the appearance of the bird that featured in the original Lowe sighting.

Since first becoming known to science in 1797, these particular birds of prey underwent an inexorable decline, to the extent that by 1987, the total world population of the species had fallen to just twenty-seven individuals. All of these survivors were then caught and formed part of what has since become a highly successful captive-breeding conservation program, with the number of California condors alive today now being in excess of 561 individuals. Some have since been released back into the wild and are starting to breed slowly in these surroundings again.

As their name suggests, however, these condors are mainly confined to the West Coast region. They were released into the Californian coastal mountains and as far south as Baja California, while further inland, they can now be found

A California condor.
Photo courtesy Agami Photo Agency/www.shutterstock.com

in northern parts of Arizona and in southern Utah. Yet given their remarkable flying abilities, there is no reason why a pair could not have flown outside their then current range in 1977 and turned up unexpectedly in a different part of North America. This is particularly likely if they were young individuals, as suggested by the dull skin coloration of their head.

There is also another, albeit far less likely explanation, based on the fact that the California condor's genus *Gymnogyps* used to consist of five species, of which this is the only known survivor. Fossil evidence has confirmed that the group used to be represented over almost the entire North American continent, reaching as far as the southeast, being present in Florida, with their distribution even extending to the Caribbean island of Cuba as well.

It does seem to be stretching the bonds of credulity just a bit far though, to suggest one of these other long-thought extinct species might still survive and account for sightings in Illinois and elsewhere over the course of the past century. Yet what this does confirm is that these birds could easily survive in other parts of the United States, especially in view of their diet as scavengers, feeding on carrion, which could account for the dead rat one individual dropped and was later retrieved by the police. It is possible that condors may occasionally actively hunt as well: a characteristic that is particularly well-recognized in the case of the Andean species. This could therefore explain the attack on Marlon Lowe.

Similarities with a Thunderbird

If a California condor was involved in this case, the chances are that it may have been a young bird, because their heads become more brightly colored with age, and this was not listed as a feature in the case of any of the sightings. If it was having difficulty in finding food, this may have been a trigger for the attack. Young birds may have been blown or driven off course to an area where they would not normally be seen. Furthermore, when California condors were more common, they would undertake regular migration flights. It could just be that the urge for this pair to do so may have resulted in them straying away from their more familiar surroundings.

Back in the 1970s, there were so few of these majestic birds of prey still left alive that very few people, even in areas which they regularly frequented, would have been used to seeing them. In contrast, the turkey vulture (or "turkey buzzard" as it is often described locally) is well-known, and it seems unlikely that many witnesses would have been fooled into thinking the mysterious sightings were down to these birds.

It is worth looking back into the ornithological records, at the behavior of California condors when the species was far more numerous. The extensive distance of 60 miles (97 km) between different sightings is unlikely to represent a significant barrier, given that they can fly at speeds up to 56 miles per hour (90 kph) and have been documented as traveling as far as 160 miles (250 km) in a single day. Another aspect of their biology, which is significant, is the fact that they do not need to feed on a daily basis, and this may explain why they were not observed to eat, with the possible exception of the reported rat.

Their flight pattern also provides a means of identification, because although California Condors flap their wings to gain lift and take off, they will then glide once they are airborne. Taking this back to native American legends about thunderbirds, it explains why they are recorded near high rocky cliffs, as the air currents here, known as thermals, help to keep these large birds airborne with minimum effort. In addition, by roosting on these high vantage points—the nearest land areas to clouds—the birds can take off more easily, benefiting from the up-current provided by the thermals. They also nest in this type of environment as well. It is quite easy to appreciate how these gigantic birds would leave their cliff-tops and descend to lower levels, appearing almost to live in the clouds.

The Case for the Turkey Vulture

The turkey vulture is one of five New World species that are grouped with the condors to form the family Cathartidae. This particular bird of prey occurs over a broader area than any other New World vulture, and it can be encountered in a correspondingly extensive range of different habitats. It also has a bright red head set against its pale bill, which is a very distinctive feature, while its wingspan is smaller than that of the California condor, reaching up to a maximum of about 6 feet (1.8 m). These birds are very well-known across the Americas, being divided into five subspecies, with two of these ranging widely across the United States.

A very conspicuous feature of the turkey vulture, especially when viewed from below in flight, is the much paler flight feathers and underside of the tail, compared with darker plumage elsewhere. These characteristics were not described by any of the witnesses who observed the mysterious birds in flight in parts of Illinois, and as mentioned, a number of these observers were very familiar with turkey vultures in any event and would have had no difficulty in recognizing them.

It therefore seems very unlikely, taking into account the size difference, that turkey vultures would have been involved in these cases, in spite of this being given as the official explanation for the various encounters and sightings that took place in Illinois. Other than California condors, however, it seems impossible to find any other explanation for these events—aside from an unrecognized species of giant bird, for which there is no evidence. Even allowing for those sparsely populated and largely unexplored areas of the United States that still exist, it seems highly unlikely in such a populous country with so many outdoor enthusiasts that an unknown bird of this type could have eluded people for so long.

A Different Explanation

Setting aside true-life encounters, however, could the origins of thunderbirds lie in another time and place? Some of the areas where they reputedly roamed were indisputably home to giants, albeit from millions of years ago. The rock formations of the American West contain some of the most significant finds of dinosaur fossils that have been unearthed in North America. They started to become prominent in the nineteenth century, with teams of excavators quarrying them out of the ground.

Long before their arrival, however, weathering meant that over the course of millennia, some of these strange and often massive bone-like structures appeared above the ground. These may have helped to inspire belief and folklore about thunderbirds among the local tribespeople. As hunter-gathers, they would certainly have recognized these remains as originating from animals. It has even been suggested that they would have been able to identify the fossils of pterosaurs as being winged creatures of huge size. Pterosaurs are in fact the largest flying animals ever to take to the skies, with wingspans of up to 36 feet (11 m), based on current finds.

It seems unlikely that pterosaurs themselves were directly responsible for thunderbird legends dating back many millennia though, because their remains would probably not have been sufficiently discernible from those of dinosaurs in the ground. Pterosaur fossils are much rarer in any case, because the skeletons of these flying reptiles are more fragile and less likely to be fossilized than those of most dinosaurs. It was not even until 1880 that the first remains of a pterosaur in the United States became known to science, thanks to the famous fossil-hunter Othniel Charles Marsh (1831–1899).

Monstrous Birds Elsewhere

Tales of giant birds in literature extend back centuries, with the most well-known being the roc, which arose from Arab legends dating back many centuries and probably originated from sailors' stories. The Venetian explorer Marco Polo (c. 1254–1324), who traveled across Asia to China, provided a description of the roc and indicated where it is likely to have lived. He described it as being a huge eagle, capable of picking up an elephant in its talons, which it would then drop on to the ground, killing the unfortunate creature, before descending to feed on its remains. Its feathers were so long that they were the equivalent of twelve paces, or approximately 36 feet (11 m).

It is unclear as to where Marco Polo gained his information, but certainly the story of the roc featured in the ancient folktales of the area of Asia through which he traveled, and they seemingly date back centuries. These were originally referred to as *One Thousand and One Nights* but became better known in the English translation simply as *The Arabian Nights*, being first published in this form in the early 1700s.

The story featuring the roc is based on a fictional character called Sinbad the sailor, who was credited with traveling widely by ship, undertaking seven voyages in the seas to the east of Africa, and encountering a range of different monsters on his adventures. This particular tale appears to have been one of the later stories added to the compendium, with the roc making its first appearance in Sinbad's second voyage, when it was encountered on a tropical island. Marco Polo reported how the roc would apparently migrate from southern latitudes to Mogadishu, the capital of Somalia, which was at that time a leading commercial and political center for the Horn of Africa.

It is generally believed that the country of origin for the legend of the roc was, however, Madagascar, an island in the Indian Ocean that was home to various megafauna that did not exist on the mainland. This phenomenon is called island gigantism and occurred, for example, in lemurs, a group of primates of which a hundred diverse species are still to be found exclusively on Madagascar, although sadly, the giant species have been hunted to extinction. Another was the carnivore known as the giant fossa (*Cryptoprocta spela*).

Nor of course was it just mammals that grew large in relative isolation from their mainland relatives, as Madagascar was home to elephant birds, which formed the Order Aepyornithiformes. The biggest—recognized by science as *Vorombe titan*—was among the largest birds, possibly *the* largest, ever to have existed, with a weight estimated as being up to 1,895 pounds (860 kg), while standing almost 10 feet (3 m) tall. It is unclear exactly when these avian giants became extinct, but certainly, they lived for a period alongside people. Furthermore, they produced giant eggs that could be up to 16 inches (40 cm) long, being the biggest ever recorded for any land vertebrate of recent times. The remains of their eggs could be found scattered widely around the landscape, reinforcing the impression to visitors that this was a land of giants.

A second avian species that used to live on Madagascar also served to reinforce the myth of the roc. Known as the Madagascar crowned hawk-eagle (*Stephanoaetus mahery*), it disappeared probably about 1500 CE, not because of direct hunting pressure but as a result of the loss of its prey, which were giant lemurs. These primates were also a favored food source of local people, and this competition for food ultimately led to the bird's extinction. These magnificent eagles were related to the crowned hawk-eagle (*S. coronatus*), which is still found on the African mainland, but they were significantly larger in size.

It is interesting that much farther away, a similar arrangement of giant birds existed on the island of New Zealand, which was home to a range of flightless giant moas, as well as the largest eagle ever known, called Haast's eagle (*Hieraaetus moorei*). It is possible that the largest females weighed as much as 36 pounds (16.5 kg) and had a wingspan approaching 10 feet (3 m). All these examples of megafauna are also now extinct.

There is actually a link between the bird life of Madagascar and that of New Zealand with the gigantic elephant birds now being known to be related to the very much smaller, flightless kiwis (*Apteryx* species), which can still be found there today. Given the source of stories about the roc, it is highly unlikely that Haast's eagle would have featured in the development of this particular myth, but within its native country, similar stories did arise based on such gigantic birds.

These relate to pouakai (also sometimes written as "pou-kai"), a bird that reputedly hunted people, carrying them off in its powerful talons. Once again, its home was reputedly in the mountains, from where it would swoop down on and seize human prey in its talons. Escape was said to be impossible, with its powerful wings making a loud sound as it swooped down on its victim.

Living Possibilities?

There are accounts of gigantic bird-like creatures from all parts of the world, but in some cases, a reptilian rather than an avian identity has been proposed for them. In September 1983, an ambulance technician named James Thompson was traveling along Highway 100 in the direction of the Texas town of Harlingen when he spotted a remarkable creature flying ahead, flapping its wings about 165 feet (50 m) in front of him.

Its most distinctive feature, aside from its long tail that appeared to end in a fin, was its body, which had no feathers on it, highlighting its blackish-gray skin. Thompson was so perplexed that he pulled over to the side of the road to get a better view. Unfortunately, this was in the days before camera phones, but he was able to estimate its size from that of the ambulance, calculating its wingspan as being approximately 6.5 feet (2 m), with a body length of between 8 and 10 feet (2.5–3 m).

What makes this encounter more compelling is that there was a report in the same period of a very similar creature, from the vicinity of Houston, roughly 300 miles (485 km) from Harlingen. On this occasion, two friends spotted what appeared to be a creature that was of almost identical appearance. Based on their description, it was comparable to the Harlingen sighting, both bringing to mind the image of a pterosaur—a representative of the lineage of flying reptiles thought to have been extinct since the end of the Age of Dinosaurs, about sixty-six million years ago. There had been an earlier report in February 1976, again from Texas, made by three teachers who were driving in a remote area to the southwest of San Antonio. They saw what they described as a huge flying creature with membranous wings, which cast a shadow across the road. It was estimated to have a wingspan of 16–20 feet (5–6 m).

It seems almost inconceivable that pterosaurs of any type could still be alive and living undetected in the skies, particularly in North America. These are not generally small, inconspicuous creatures, nor do they live in the depths of the oceans, where, like coelacanths (see page 5), they could hide away. If pterosaurs were still alive undetected on the planet, the chances are that their relic population would survive in a much remoter corner of wilderness.

Two Puzzling Cases

Interestingly, there have in fact been reports of pterosaur-type creatures from Papua New Guinea. Two distinctive types are recognized by local people. The larger form is known locally as the "duah," or sometimes as the "duwas," and is said to have a wingspan of 20–23 feet (6–7 m). The smaller "ropen," with a wingspan estimated at about half this size, is said to be confined to just two small islands. These are Umboi, which is located off the eastern coast of New Guinea, near New Britain and Rambutyo, which lies some distance to the north, forming part of the Admiralty Islands archipelago, to the east of Manus.

There seems to be a tradition surrounding both creatures, in terms of native accounts, which treat them both as living entities, rather than mythological beings. Various residents who claimed to be familiar with the duah have stated that these flying creatures were more common fifty years ago, when they could be seen flying in small flocks, typically at night, whereas nowadays, they are much rarer, with individuals usually to be seen on their own. Their nocturnal lifestyle does suggest they could possibly be a species of bat that is currently unrecognized by science, however—a theory reinforced by the fact that duahs are believed to inhabit caves.

Nevertheless, the reported wingspan of the duah makes it far larger than any known type of bat. The Pacific region is home to the fruit-eating flying foxes, which rank as some of the biggest bats in the world. The golden-crowned flying fox, which is to be found in the Philippines, has a wingspan measuring up to 5.6 feet (1.7 m) overall, making it the largest known bat, but this would still be much smaller than in the case of the duah.

The identity of a bat would better-suit the ropen, in terms of its size. According to accounts from the island, these creatures have teeth in their mouths and what has been described as an enlarged, diamond-shaped tip to the tail. They too live in caves when not out searching for food. Interestingly, they have been recorded as grabbing fish from the catches of local fishermen, rather like the various fish-eating bats that swoop down and seize fish in flight from the surface of the water, using their powerful feet to gain a grip on their target. It seems more likely that these sightings can be explained on this basis, rather than by the survival of flying reptiles thought to have become extinct about sixty-six million years ago, although the identity of the duah is undoubtedly harder to explain.

No Clear Answers

It is surprisingly easy to mistake the size of a bird, especially one seen from some distance away, when it is flying in the sky with no clear point of reference. Equally, there are a number of birds that, by virtue of their size or profile, could be confused with a likely impression of a pterosaur in flight, ranging from storks to cormorants.

Meanwhile, thunderbird sightings and reports continue to be made in various parts of North America, including Alaska, to the present day. Multiple sightings were reported from Pennsylvania in 2024, notably in the vicinity of South Greensburg on May 22, when a large, dark-colored bird was seen by various observers. More recently, a video purporting to be of a thunderbird, with a pterosaur-like appearance, was captured on June 16, 2025, at the Rocky Rover reservation in Ohio. This mystery has yet to be solved.

Ten Things You May Not Know About Thunderbirds

1   Thunderbird Field is a famous military airfield located in Glendale, Arizona, which was used to train pilots during the Second World War (1939–1945). It was funded by various Hollywood stars of the period, including James Stewart, Henry Fonda, and his wife, Margaret Sullavan.

2   A second Thunderbird Field, designated #2, was created in 1942 at nearby Scottsdale.

3   The site was designed by the architectural designer Millard Sheets, so that from the air, it reflects the outline of a thunderbird created

by the Ancestral Pueblo people, who lived in parts of Utah, Arizona, New Mexico, and Colorado.

4   The hugely popular sci-fi television series known as *Thunderbirds* was named by its creator Gerry Anderson after this airfield, simply because his brother Lionel had been based there.

5   Thunderbird, being the costumed character of John Proudstar, was featured in Marvel Comic publications. He was a rare superhero, being an Apache Native American. After the character was killed off, he was resurrected forty-five years later, featuring in *X-Men: The Trial of Magneto #5* in 2021.

6   The Ford Thunderbird was a very popular North American car that began life as a two-seater convertible in 1955, with a second row of seats being added three years later. It remained in production until 1997 and was then marketed again from 2002 to 2005. In total, more than 4.4 million of these cars were sold, and it became popularly known as the T-Bird.

7   Sports teams around the world have adopted the name of Thunderbirds. They include the Seattle Thunderbirds, a US ice hockey team; the Adelaide Thunderbirds, an Australian netball team; and the Thunderbird Soccer Club, which is based in Taiwan.

8   Various motorcycles made by companies such as Triumph and Royal Enfield have been given the description of Thunderbird as part of their name, presumably to reflect their power.

9   An early seaplane, manufactured in Glendale, California, was called the Thunderbird W-14. Somewhere between forty and fifty of these planes were produced before the company that made them went bankrupt.

10 The US Air Force includes a demonstration squadron known as the Thunderbirds, with a long history extending back to 1917.

Further Readings

Introduction

Alderton, David. *Breakfast with a Bigfoot* (London: Beaver Books (Hutchinson), 1986).
Redfern, Nick. *The Monster Book: Creatures, Beasts and Fiends of Nature* (Detroit, MI: Visible Ink Press, 2016).

1. The Quest for the Unicorn

Hathaway, Nancy. *The Unicorn* (New York: Viking Press, 1980).
Lavers, Chris. *The Natural History of Unicorns* (London: Granta Publications, 2009).
Mayor, Adrienne. *The First Fossil Hunters: Dinosaurs, Mammoths, and Myth in Greek and Roman Times* (Princeton, NJ: Princeton University Press, 2000 and updated 2020).
Savery, Annabel. *Unicorns: Magic, Myth, and Mystery* (London: Franklin Watts, 2019).
Shepard, Odell. *The Lore of the Unicorn* (Boston, MA: Houghton Mifflin,1930).
Turgeon, Carolyn. *The Unicorn Handbook* (New York: Harper Design (Harper Collins) 2020).

2. Mermaids and Mermen

Alexander, Skye. *Mermaids: The Myths, Legends, and Lore* (Avon, MA: Adams Media, 2012).
Hansen, William (ed.). *The Book of Greek & Roman Folktales, Legends & Myths* (Princeton, NJ: Princeton University Press, 2017).
Ratisseau, Elizabeth. *Mermaids and Mermen: Legends of the Sea* (New York: MetroBooks, 1999).
Scribner, Vaughn. *Merpeople: A Human History* (London: Reaktion Books, 2020).
Stine, R. L. *Mermaids: Myth or Reality?* (New York: Scholastic Book Services, 1978).

3. The World of Dragons

Arnold, Martin. *The Dragon: Fear and Power* (London: Reaktion Books, 2018).
Chamberlain, Basil Hall. *A Translation of the "Ko-ji-ki" or Records of Ancient Matters* (Yokohama, Japan: R. Meiklejohn, 1882).
Evans, Jonathan D. *Dragons: Myth and Legend*, (Edison, NJ: Chartwell Books, 2008).
Ingersoll, Ernest. *Dragons and Dragon Lore* (New York: Payson & Clarke, 1928).

Johansson, Björn K. *The Book of Dragons* (independently published: available through Amazon, 2024).

Jones, David E. *An Instinct for Dragons* (New York: Routledge, 2000).

Niles, Doug. *Dragons—The Myths, Legends & Lore* (Avon, MA: Adams Media (F&W Media Inc.), 2013).

Shuker, Karl. *Dragons: A Natural History* (New York: Simon & Schuster, New York 1995).

Welch, Patricia Bjaaland. *Chinese Art: A Guide to Motifs and Visual Imagery* (North Clarendon, VT: Tuttle Publishing, 2008).

Yang, Lihui, Deming An, Jessica Anderson Turner. *Handbook of Chinese Mythology* (Oxford: Oxford University Press, 2005).

4. The Rise of the Phoenix

Barber, Richard. Bestiary: Being an English Version of the Bodleian Library, Oxford M.S. Bodley 764 (Woodbridge, UK: Boydell Press, 1993).

Frigiola, Heather. *Monsters and Mythical Creatures from Around the World* (Atglen, PA: Red Feather, Mind, Body, Spirit (Schiffer Publishing) 2019).

Nigg, Joseph. *The Phoenix: An Unnatural Biography of a Mythical Beast* (Chicago, IL: University of Chicago Press, 2016).

Reese, M. R. *The Phoenix in Myth and Legend* (Wellingborough, UK: Aquarian Press, 1988).

5. Vanquishing Vampires

Barber, Paul. *Vampires, Burial, and Death: Folklore and Reality* (New Haven, CT: Yale University Press, 1988).

Cheung, Theresa. *The Element Encyclopedia of Vampires: An A–Z of the Undead* (London, UK: Harper Element (Harper Collins Publishers), 2009).

Montague, Charlotte. *Vampires: The Complete Guide to Vampire Mythology* (London: Sphere (Little, Brown Book Group), 2010).

Nuzum, Eric. *The Dead Travel Fast: Stalking Vampires from Nosferatu to Count Chocula.* (New York: Thomas Dunne Books (St. Martin's Press), 2007).

Overstreet, Deborah Wilson. *Not Your Mother's Vampire: Vampires in Young Adult Fiction* (Lanham, MD: Scarecrow Press, 2006).

Suckling, Nigel. *Vampires* (London: Facts, Figures & Fun (AAPPL Artists" and Photographers' Press), 2006).

Summers, Montague. *The Vampire: His Kith and Kin* (London: Kegan Paul, Trench, Trubner & Co, 1928).

Wright, Dudley. *Vampires & Vampirism—Legends from Around the World* (Maple Shade, NJ: Lethe Press, 2001).

6. The Curse of Werewolves and Dogmen

Baring-Gould, Sabine. *The Book of Were-Wolves: Being an Account of a Terrible Superstition* (Mineola, NY: Dover Publications, 2006 reprint (first edition 1865)).

Godfrey, Linda S. *Real Wolfmen: True Encounters in Modern America* (New York: TarcherPerigee (Penguin Random House), 2012).

Godfrey, Linda S. *American Werewolves: The True Story of the Dogman* (New York: TarcherPerigee (Penguin Random House), 2020).

Steiger, Brad. *The Werewolf Book: The Encyclopedia of Shape-Shifting Beings* (Detroit, MI: Visible Ink Press, 1999).

Suckling, Nigel. *Werewolves* (London: Facts, Figures & Fun (AAPPL Artists' and Photographers' Press), 2006).

7. Searching for Sasquatch (Bigfoot)

Bayanov, Dmitri and Christopher Murphy. *Bigfoot Research: The Russian Vision* (Surrey, BC: Hancock House Publishers, 2019).

Buhs, Joshua Blu. *Bigfoot: The Life and Times of a Legend* (Chicago, IL: University of Chicago Press, 2009).

John. *Sasquatch: The Apes Among Us* (Surrey, BC: Hancock House Publishers, 1978).

Krantz, Grover S. *Big Footprints: A Scientific Inquiry into the Reality of Sasquatch* (Boulder, CO: Johnson Books, 1992).

Redfern, Nick. *The Bigfoot Book: The Encyclopedia of Sasquatch, Yeti and Cryptic Primates* (Detroit, MI: Visible Ink Press, 2016).

Zada, John. *In the Valleys of the Noble Beyond: In Search of the Sasquatch* (New York: Atlantic Monthly Press, 2019).

8. The Thunderbird and Similar Tales

Hall, Mark A. and Loren Coleman. *Thunderbirds: America's Living Legends of Giant Birds* (New York: Paraview Press, 2004).

Mayor, Adrienne. *Fossil Legends of the First Americans* (Princeton, NJ: Princeton University Press, 2005).

Index

About the Authors

David Alderton is an award-winning author, whose books on animals and nature subjects have sold over seven million copies worldwide and are available in thirty-three languages. He trained at Cambridge University as a veterinarian, but an allergy to soaps, which developed in his final year of study, led him into media work, focusing on pets and the broader natural world, which has fascinated him from an early age. Aside from writing, David frequently takes part in radio and television programs about animals of all types, and he is enthusiastic about traveling. Although he has trekked in Sasquatch country, visited the supposed home of the Yowie and various other locations described in this book, he does, however, admit that the particular creatures featured here have eluded him to date! David's website can be found at www.petinfoclub.com and he has a YouTube channel @DavidAlderton-v2t to which his coauthor Akara regularly contributes. They have also created the *Amazing Animals* podcast series, which has currently attracted a large audience in sixty-two countries worldwide.

Akara Heart has always been drawn to the arts and has pursued training in acting, dancing, and presenting. She has performed in feature films and at festivals, and frequently collaborates with David Alderton on various film, podcasting, and written projects. These include being commissioned by SriLankan Airlines to script and co-present a film as well as a book about the unique annual elephant migration that takes place on the island. Akara resides in Glastonbury in the west of England, where, in addition to writing, creating stories and digital artworks, she holds regular sacred dance workshops and courses, and also works as a freelance photographer. In her free time, she enjoys leisurely walks in Avalon with Halo, her beloved PomChi. Akara's website can be found at www.sacredtemplearts.co.uk and @akaraheart333 is her YouTube channel.